PROMOTE YOURSELF
WITH BETTER GRAMMAR

...to better grades ...better schools ...better impressions ...a better career

Copyright © 2000 by Elizabeth M. McFadden.
Published by Manpower Education Institute • 715 Ladd Road, Bronx, NY 10471-1203
phone 718-548-4200 • fax: 718-548-4202 • e-mail: meiready@aol.com
www.manpower-education.org • www.bettergrammar.org

With the generous support of Verizon and Channel 4 WNBC, we've prepared this handy book and accompanying Web site to help you improve your everyday use of English.

In the end, we hope your prospects in your career and in your schoolwork, along with your self-confidence, will soar.

Theodore W. Kheel
Workforce Distance Learning Foundation

James J. McFadden
Manpower Education Institute

This book is dedicated to the next generation of writers—in particular, Amber and Megan, young communicators who enjoy writing. We hope that they will use their skills to bring joy to others through their writing, resolve disputes with thoughtful presentations, and develop meaningful friendships throughout their lives.

With heartfelt appreciation to the entire team for their dedication and inspiration:

Philip Carrano
Shirley de Leon
Kevin Delgado
Michael Grace
Barbara Howell
Carl Koch
Elizabeth McFadden

Patrick McFadden
Beth Murphy
Ann Noonan
Monsignor Daniel Peake
Loreen Ryan
Trilby Schreiber
Emery Westfall

Digital Graphic Services, Inc.
Paula McDonald graphic design
and many others—you know who you are

Published in the United States of America

First Edition • ISBN 1-882548-07-8

INTRODUCTION 1

IMAGINE a city without traffic laws, with cars and pedestrians unable to move. Imagine a ball game with no rules. Chaos? Confusion?

It's the same with language. When we follow the rules and use correct grammar, we are understood. Being understood brings rewards. A grammatically correct paper earns a higher grade. Landing that good job becomes more likely when the application and resume are written in proper English. Promotions go more readily to those who express themselves clearly.

Mastering grammar is a step-by-step process. Don't try to conquer this book all at once. Think of PROMOTE YOURSELF as both a guide and a handy reference tool. Slowly make your way through its chapters. Study the examples provided and take advantage of the practice exercises to test your skill.

As you leaf through these pages, keep in mind that you do not need to memorize every rule. More important is that you become familiar with the rules and understand them. You may already know some of them.

> "The minute you get away from the fundamentals—whether it's proper technique, work ethic, or mental preparation—the bottom can fall out of your game, your school work, your job, whatever you're doing"
>
> **Michael Jordan**

An understanding of grammar helps you evaluate your writing and improve it. As you gain command of the fundamental concepts presented in this book, you'll be able to avoid making the embarrassing grammatical mistakes that can hold you back. Your personal confidence will soar as you become accustomed to using language properly.

NOUNS

A noun names a { **PERSON, PLACE, THING, or IDEA.**

TYPE OF NOUN	WHAT IT DOES OR WHAT IT IS	EXAMPLES
common noun	• names any person, place, thing, or idea	woman city magazine politics
proper noun	• names a particular person, place, thing, or idea • always begins with a capital letter	Christina Chicago Newsweek Middle Ages
concrete noun	• names an object that occupies space or can be recognized by any of the senses	table computer sound scent
abstract noun	• names an idea, a quality, or a characteristic	loyalty freshness beauty grace
collective noun	• names a group	committee family troop band
compound noun	• a noun made from two or more words • may be open, hyphenated or closed	insurance company follow-up commander-in-chief heartache sidewalk

PLURAL NOUNS

Nouns can be **singular** or **plural**.

Singular means **one** person, place, thing, or idea.

Plural means **more than one** person, place, thing, or idea.

ENDING	WHAT TO DO	SINGULAR	PLURAL
most nouns	add s	girl town	girls towns
vowel and y	add s	boy turkey	boys turkeys
vowel and o	add s	radio rodeo	radios rodeos
s, x, z, ch, sh	add es	glass waltz dish	glasses waltzes dishes
consonant and y	change y to i and add es	city lady	cities ladies
consonant and o	usually add es	potato echo	potatoes echoes
consonant and o	sometimes add s	zero photo	zeros photos
f or fe	usually change f to v add s or es	wife half thief	wives halves thieves
f or fe	sometimes add s	roof cliff giraffe	roofs cliffs giraffes
some nouns	change form	foot child mouse	feet children mice

POSSESSIVE NOUNS

A **possessive noun** shows who or what **owns** something.

To make a singular noun possessive, add an **apostrophe** and an **s ('s)**.

To form the possessive of plural nouns that do not end in s, add an **apostrophe** and an **s ('s)**.

To make plural nouns possessive, add an **apostrophe (')**.

EXAMPLES:

girl	girl's	I like that girl's hair.
family	family's	That is my family's car.
children	children's	I swam in the children's pool.
people	people's	This is the people's park.
girls	girls'	Where is the girls' locker room?
families	families'	Our families' parties are fun.

NOTE: *To see more rules concerning possessive nouns see page 72.*

PRACTICE

Identify each underlined word as either a common noun or a proper noun.

EXAMPLE: <u>Mrs. Jones</u> lives in that house. ANSWER: proper noun

1. The car <u>lights</u> are turned off.
2. The new car belongs to <u>Doctor Riley</u>.
3. The lesson <u>Jeanne</u> studied was very interesting.
4. Is this <u>restaurant</u> closed?
5. The <u>teacher</u> spoke with me.

Add 's or ' to each noun to show ownership.

EXAMPLE: Their <u>family</u> vacation was fun.
ANSWER: Their <u>family's</u> vacation was fun.

6. Some <u>people</u> voices can always be heard.
7. That store sells <u>women</u> shoes.
8. Where are his <u>grandchildren</u> toys?
9. <u>Gus</u> car is being repaired.
10. The <u>birds</u> nests are empty.

Add s or es to make each noun plural.

EXAMPLE: street ANSWER: streets

11. parade
12. fox
13. room
14. bush
15. beach

Change each noun to its plural form.

EXAMPLE: family ANSWER: families

16. goose
17. housefly
18. man
19. party
20. tooth

PRONOUNS 3

A **pronoun** is used instead of a noun. The word or group of words to which a pronoun refers is its **antecedent**.

EXAMPLES: My mother baked a cake. (Mother and cake are nouns.)
She baked it. (She and it are pronouns.)

Pronouns can be **singular** or **plural**.

The singular pronoun refers to one person, place, thing, or idea.
EXAMPLES: I, it

The plural pronoun refers to more than one person, place, thing, or idea.
EXAMPLES: we, they

SOME OTHER PRONOUNS

he	his	me	them	this	which
him	I	mine	their	us	who
her	it	she	theirs	we	you
hers	its	that	they	what	yours

PERSONAL PRONOUNS

A **personal pronoun** refers to a specific person, place, thing, or idea. A personal pronoun must agree with its antecedent in number.

Pronouns are said to be in the **first person** when they refer to **the speaker**.
EXAMPLES: I try my very best.
We try our very best.

Pronouns are said to be in the **second person** when they refer to **the person spoken to**.
EXAMPLES: You are a hard worker.
You are hard workers.

Pronouns are said to be in the **third person** when they refer to **the person spoken about**.
EXAMPLES: She enjoys going to school.
They enjoy going to school.

PERSONAL PRONOUNS

	SINGULAR	PLURAL
FIRST PERSON	I me	we us
SECOND PERSON	you	you
THIRD PERSON	he him she her it	they them

POSSESSIVE PRONOUNS

A possessive pronoun shows who or what **owns** something. It can be **singular** or **plural**.

The possessive pronouns **my, your, our, his, her, its,** and **their** are followed by a noun.

> EXAMPLES: My children liked the movie.
> The dog wagged its tail.

The possessive pronouns **mine, yours, hers, his, ours,** and **theirs** stand on their own.

> EXAMPLES: That pen is mine.
> The shoes are theirs.

His is a possessive pronoun, which either is followed by a noun or stands alone.

> EXAMPLES: His favorite sport is basketball.
> The tickets for the game are his.

REFLEXIVE & INTENSIVE PRONOUNS

Both reflexive and intensive pronouns end with either **self** or **selves**. These pronouns look alike but their usage is different. A **reflexive** pronoun adds information to a sentence, while an **intensive** pronoun adds emphasis to another noun or pronoun.

> EXAMPLES:

Megan taught herself to play the piano. Evan walked himself to school.	reflexive pronoun
Joc himself prepared the science project. Barbara herself came to the party.	intensive pronoun

DEMONSTRATIVE PRONOUNS

A demonstrative pronoun points out **specific** persons, places, things, or ideas.

DEMONSTRATIVE PRONOUNS		
SINGULAR	this	that
PLURAL	these	those

> EXAMPLES: This meal is delicious.
> I will buy three of those.

INTERROGATIVE PRONOUNS

An interrogative pronoun is a pronoun that is used in asking questions. There are three interrogative pronouns: **who**, **which**, and **what**. The word who has two additional forms: **whom** and **whose**.

EXAMPLES: Which do you like best?
What can I do for you?

Who is used in the subject of a sentence.

EXAMPLE: Who is your neighbor?

Whom is used as the object of the action verb.

EXAMPLE: Whom have you chosen to be captain?

Whose is a pronoun that shows ownership.

EXAMPLE: Whose voice is that?

WATCH OUT!

The word **whose** shows possession. The contraction **who's** means who is.

For more on contractions see page 73.

RELATIVE PRONOUNS

A relative pronoun serves as both a **pronoun** and a **connective** in a compound sentence (see page 38).

EXAMPLE WITHOUT RELATIVE PRONOUN: This is the lifeguard, and he saved my life.

EXAMPLES: This is the lifeguard who saved my life.
I wish it were you who had gone with us.

Who, **whose**, and **whom** refer to persons.

EXAMPLES: I know the boy who threw the snowball.
I saw the girl whom all of us admire.
This is the bell whose sound we hear.

That and **which** refer to animals, persons, things, or ideas.

EXAMPLES: This is the map that shows where we live.
The ostrich is a large bird, which does not fly.

RELATIVE PRONOUNS	
who	whoever
which	whichever
what	whatever
whom	whomever
whose	that

INDEFINITE PRONOUNS

An indefinite pronoun refers to persons, places, things, or ideas **in a more general way** than a noun does.

EXAMPLES: Everyone is going to the movies.
Several of the people saw the shooting star.
Did you know anyone at the party?

SOME INDEFINITE PRONOUNS				
all	none	many	few	any
several	both	some	much	something
everybody	everything	anybody	anything	nothing

PRACTICE

Replace the underlined word or words with a pronoun.

EXAMPLE: The children ate breakfast at 7 o'clock.   ANSWER: They ate breakfast at 7 o'clock.

1.   My sister grows tomatoes every year.
2.   The bird flew out of the nest.
3.   The boys and girls like to listen to music.
4.   Will you bring a present for Mike?
5.   Who bought Uncle Joe's baseball ticket?

Identify the underlined nouns or pronouns as first person, second person, or third person.

EXAMPLE: John has blown out all of the candles on his birthday cake.   ANSWER: third person

6.   You must learn to drive carefully.
7.   The coach taught them the merit of teamwork.
8.   I am going to sing in the concert.
9.   Will you teach me how to ski?
10. Susan has given us a lot of help.

Underline the correct possessive pronoun.

EXAMPLE: Mine/My friends are great people.   ANSWER: My friends are great people.

11. My/Mine is the last one.
12. My/Mine cat is gray.
13. Are those tickets their/theirs?
14. Its/It's sound is pleasant.
15. They/Their car is in the parking lot.

Use a relative pronoun to connect each pair of sentences.

EXAMPLE: Where is Tom? Tom delivers the mail.   ANSWER: Where is Tom who delivers the mail?

16. This is the road. The road goes to Anna's house.
17. My dog is three years old. Three years is like 21 in dog years.
18. This is my tennis coach, Mary. Mary is also my best friend.
19. The flag will be carried by a student. The student will become the class leader.
20. My juice is in a glass. The glass is on the table.

Underline the correct interrogative pronoun to complete each sentence.

EXAMPLE: Who/Whom is coming to see you?   ANSWER: <u>Who</u> is coming to see you?

21. Who/Whom are you seeing today?

22. Who/Whom did you invite to the party?

23. Who/Whose work is complete?

24. Did you find out who/whom gave you the tickets for the game?

25. Who/Whom was he trying to call?

26. What/Which of the colors matches your eyes?

27. Who/Whom scored the winning run?

28. Who/What is your name?

29. Who/Whom invented the radio?

30. Who/Whom did you ask?

31. Who/Whose idea was that?

Underline the pronoun in each sentence and identify what type of pronoun it is: personal, possessive, reflexive, intensive, demonstrative, or indefinite.

EXAMPLE: Their team won second place.

ANSWER: <u>Their</u> team won second place. (possessive)

32. This is a favorite photo.

33. Tony will go the store himself.

34. Her dog does tricks.

35. Does anyone want milk?

36. Laura herself fixed the leak.

37. Bernie has two of those at home.

38. They are always together.

39. Something is wrong with the telephone.

40. Their car is green.

41. Which one did Wendy buy?

42. We are lab partners.

43. That movie was scary.

VERBS

> A verb is a word that expresses } **ACTION or BEING.**

ACTION VERBS

An action verb tells what someone or something does that is either **physical** or **mental**.

PHYSICAL ACTION: walk, jump, dance
MENTAL ACTION: think, study, like

TRANSITIVE & INTRANSITIVE VERBS

A verb that expresses action can be a transitive verb or an intransitive verb.

A **transitive verb** is an action verb that is followed by a word or words (the direct object) that answer the question **what** or **whom**. The direct object is the noun or pronoun that receives the action of the verb (see page 28).

EXAMPLE: The boy hit the ball.

TRANSITIVE VERB   DIRECT OBJECT

An **intransitive verb** is an action verb that is **not** followed by a word that answers the question **what** or **whom**. No noun or pronoun receives any action. An intransitive verb does not take a direct object (see page 28).

EXAMPLES: The wind blew.   The airplane landed.   Birds sing.
            Children laugh.   The horse jumped.

Some verbs can be transitive or intransitive depending upon their usage.

EXAMPLES:

The boy returned the money. TRANSITIVE VERB DIRECT OBJECT The boy returned. INTRANSITIVE VERB	The direct object answers the question, **what** did the boy return?
Mary sang the National Anthem. TRANSITIVE VERB DIRECT OBJECT Mary sang. INTRANSITIVE VERB	The direct object answers the question, **what** did Mary sing?

BEING OR LINKING VERBS

A being or linking verb **joins** the subject of a sentence (a noun or pronoun) with a word or expression that identifies or describes the subject (a noun, a pronoun, or an adjective).

The verb **be** and all its forms are the most common linking verbs. A being verb expresses **a state of existence or condition**.

FORMS OF THE VERB BE	
am	were
is	being
are	been
was	

OTHER VERBS THAT EXPRESS CONDITION		
feel	grow	taste
seem	look	remain
appear	turn	smell
become	stay	sound

EXAMPLES: The cake tastes good.
You look marvelous!
Angela is smart.
The music sounds wonderful.

VERB PHRASES

A verb phrase is a **group of words** used as the verb in a sentence. A verb phrase consists of the **main verb and all its auxiliary verbs**. Auxiliary verbs include forms of **be** and **have**. In a verb phrase, the auxiliary verb (also known as helping verb) helps other verbs to express time or emphasize meaning. The auxiliary verb comes first in a verb phrase.

FORMS OF THE VERB HAVE	
has	had
have	having

OTHER AUXILIARY VERBS			
can	does	might	should
could	did	must	will
do	may	shall	would

EXAMPLES:

	AUXILIARY VERB(S)	VERB
You will see.	will	see
The tree has fallen.	has	fallen
We might have invited her.	might have	invited
Your mail has been delivered.	has been	delivered

PRACTICE

Underline the verb in each sentence.

> EXAMPLE: The ball rolled into the neighbor's yard.
> ANSWER: The ball <u>rolled</u> into the neighbor's yard.

1.   All of us enjoy your stories.
2.   You read many books this summer!
3.   We ride the same bus to school every day.
4.   I think about you often.
5.   Their family swims at the beach in August.
6.   The patient feels much better today.
7.   We have been out for most of the day.
8.   Dim lights appeared through the fog.
9.   I was at the game last night.
10.   The juniors and seniors are in the auditorium.

Underline the auxiliary verb in each sentence.

> EXAMPLE: Jessica will travel to Rome this summer.
> ANSWER: Jessica <u>will</u> travel to Rome this summer.

11.   Kelly is studying for her next exam.
12.   Carrie has driven the blue car for two years.
13.   Chris can visit his parents every weekend.
14.   Your car was towed away.
15.   I am trying this new recipe.

Underline the verb phrase in each sentence.

> EXAMPLE: We shall finish our baseball game before four o'clock.
> ANSWER: We <u>shall finish</u> our baseball game before four o'clock.

16.   I must send those packages soon.
17.   The manager will close the store early today.
18.   She has been digging in her garden all afternoon.
19.   He has heard that story before.
20.   Anthony has closed the door.

Underline the verb in each sentence and identify it as transitive or intransitive.

EXAMPLE: Brian raised his hand when he knew the answers.

ANSWER: Brian <u>raised</u> his hand when he knew the answers. (transitive)

21. The lost child sobbed in the corner of the store.

22. Mrs. Griffin pushed the baby carriage down the street.

23. They ran for hours.

24. The squirrels gathered acorns for their young.

25. We grew many different vegetables in the garden.

26. The snow fell.

27. Her children never share their toys.

28. The band marched in the parade.

29. The children slept.

30. The author sold many books.

Underline the object of each transitive verb.

EXAMPLE: The baker dropped the hot bread.

ANSWER: The baker dropped the hot <u>bread</u>.

31. The contractors built a new house.

32. I met the man of my dreams at the party.

33. The porter carried the old woman's luggage.

34. The river flooded the farmer's fields.

35. She chose her best friend as her bridesmaid.

Underline the linking verb in each sentence.

EXAMPLE: Murder mysteries are my favorite books.

ANSWER: Murder mysteries <u>are</u> my favorite books.

36. The strawberries tasted so sweet.

37. I was ready for the trip.

38. The lilacs in the garden smell sweet.

39. Jack felt nervous about his trip.

40. Mr. McGurn is an editor of a daily newspaper.

5 ADJECTIVES

An ADJECTIVE describes a NOUN or PRONOUN.

An adjective is a word that describes or modifies a noun or a pronoun. It tells **what kind**, **how many**, **which one**, or **how much**. An adjective usually comes just before the noun or pronoun it describes.

EXAMPLES:

	ADJECTIVE(S)	NOUN DESCRIBED
Look at that small dog!	small	dog
A wise person listens carefully.	wise	person
Many people attended the concert.	Many	people
Will you lend me twenty dollars?	twenty	dollars
Mildred put ten red roses on the table.	ten red	roses

PROPER ADJECTIVES

A proper adjective is formed from a proper noun. A proper adjective begins with a capital letter.

EXAMPLES: American citizen   Chinese food   African forests   English language

POSSESSIVE ADJECTIVES

Possessive nouns and pronouns are considered adjectives because they modify nouns.

EXAMPLES: Joseph's painting   her friend   our pet

PREDICATE ADJECTIVES

A predicate adjective describes the subject of a sentence and follows a linking verb.

EXAMPLES:

	SUBJECT	LINKING VERB	PREDICATE ADJECTIVE
The game was long.	game	was	long
I feel pretty.	I	feel	pretty

ARTICLES

Articles are the adjectives **a**, **an**, and **the**.

A and **an** are called **indefinite articles**. **A** is used before consonant sounds, and **an** is used before vowel sounds.

The is called a **definite article**.

EXAMPLES OF ARTICLES

the book	a book	an open book
the hat	a hat	a wool hat
the test	a test	an easy test
the glass	a glass	an empty glass
the man	a man	an honest man
the umbrella	an umbrella	a black umbrella

COMPARING WITH ADJECTIVES

To compare nouns with each other, three adjective forms are used: the positive form, the comparative form, and the superlative form.

The **positive** form of an adjective shows quality only and does not compare one noun to another.

    EXAMPLES: That tree is tall.
                     Mom's food tastes delicious.

The **comparative** form of an adjective compares the qualities of two nouns. When an adjective compares nouns, we often add **er** to the positive form of the adjective. For adjectives with several syllables, the adverbs **more** or **less** are used.

    INCORRECT: The house is more taller than the tree.
    CORRECT: The house is taller than the tree.
                    Math is more complicated than English.

The **superlative** form of an adjective compares the qualities of more than two nouns. When an adjective compares more than two nouns, we often add **est** to the positive form of the adjective. For adjectives with several syllables, the adverbs **most** or **least** are used.

    INCORRECT: The most loudest band lost the competition.
    CORRECT: The loudest band lost the competition.
                    The most unusual animals are in the zoo.

POSITIVE	COMPARATIVE	SUPERLATIVE
nice	nicer	nicest
beautiful	more beautiful	most beautiful
generous	less generous	least generous

WATCH OUT!

Never use **er** with **more** or **less**.

Never use **est** with **most** or **least**.

Several adjectives change their form when used to compare nouns or pronouns.

POSITIVE	COMPARATIVE	SUPERLATIVE
good	better	best
bad	worse	worst
some	more	most

    EXAMPLES: There are some cookies on the table.
                    There are more cookies in the cookie jar.
                    The most cookies I have ever seen are in the bakery.

PRACTICE

Underline the adjective or adjectives in each sentence

EXAMPLE: The sky was filled with dark clouds.   ANSWER: The sky was filled with <u>dark</u> clouds.

1.   I bought a new green hat.
2.   Mary's blue dress is stunning.
3.   Some people will help you.
4.   The red flowers are on the kitchen table.
5.   It was the worst storm of the decade.
6.   The farthest distance he ran was ten miles.

Underline the adjective in each sentence and identify it as a possessive adjective, a predicate adjective, or a proper adjective.

EXAMPLE: We studied Indian legends about animals.
ANSWER: We studied <u>Indian</u> legends about animals. (proper adjective)

7.   I love Swiss chocolate.
8.   This stew is great!
9.   Our house has a fireplace.
10. We went to a Hawaiian luau.
11. Laura's book is damaged.
12. Will he stay long?

Underline the adjectives in the sentences below and identify each one as a positive, comparative, or superlative adjective.

EXAMPLE: Mary Kate is older than her sister.
ANSWER. Mary Kate is <u>older</u> than her sister. (comparative adjective)

13. The most beautiful sunsets are seen on a beach.
14. The truth sounds stranger than fiction.
15   That is a pretty dress.
16. Your first project was more difficult than this one.
17. Are you looking for a better job?
18. Thank you for the hot meal.
19. Andy wore his oldest clothes to clean the attic.
20. The musician felt more frustrated today than yesterday.
21. Jimmy was about to face the most difficult challenge of his life.
22. The lamp has a tinted shade.

An **ADVERB** describes a VERB, an ADJECTIVE, or another ADVERB.

An adverb is a word **that** describes or modifies a **verb**, an **adjective**, or another **adverb**. Adverbs modify verbs much as adjectives modify nouns.

EXAMPLES:

	ADJECTIVE	NOUN
The bright light flashed in the window.	bright	light
The slow boat went up the river.	slow	boat
The beautiful flower grew in the garden.	beautiful	flower

	ADVERB	VERB
The light flashed brightly in the window.	brightly	flashed
The boat went slowly up the river.	slowly	went
The flower grew beautifully in the garden.	beautifully	grew

An adverb tells **how**, **where**, **when**, or **to what degree**. Adverbs usually modify verbs or adjectives. Most adverbs end in **ly**.

An adverb which answers the question
{ **how** usually modifies a verb or an adjective, rarely an adverb.
when usually modifies a verb.
where usually modifies a verb.
to what degree modifies a verb, an adjectives, or an adverb.

EXAMPLES:

	ADVERB(S)	TELLS	MODIFIES
The snow fell softly and silently.	softly silently	how	fell (verb)
The pain was terribly severe.	terribly	how	severe (adjective)
He was recently promoted.	recently	when	promoted (verb)
Come here.	here	where	come (verb)
John studied upstairs.	upstairs	where	studied (verb)
Carrie completely forgot that.	completely	degree	forgot (verb)
Matthew is very tall.	very	degree	tall (adjective)
She moved quite carefully.	quite	degree	carefully (adverb)
	carefully	how	moved (verb)

INTERROGATIVE ADVERBS

Interrogative adverbs are often used to introduce a question. These include **how**, **when**, **where**, and **why**.

EXAMPLES: How did you get here?
When do you expect to return?
Where are you going?
Why did you come?

NEGATIVE WORDS AS ADVERBS

The word **not** and the contraction **n't** are considered adverbs.

> EXAMPLES: That is not possible.
> They haven't left the building.

Never, **no**, **nowhere**, and **hardly** can function as adverbs of time, place, and degree.

COMPARING WITH ADVERBS

Adverbs, like adjectives, have three different forms to show the degree of comparison. The forms are the positive form, the comparative form, and the superlative form.

The **positive form** of an adverb shows quality only and does not compare one action to another.

> EXAMPLES: Ann successfully completed the test.
> Erin ran fast.

The **comparative form** of an adverb compares two actions. To create the comparative form, add **er**. For most adverbs with two or more syllables, add **more**.

> EXAMPLES: Tom runs faster than Mary.
> The tortoise moves more slowly than the hare.

The **superlative form** of an adverb compares more than two actions. To create the superlative form, add **est**. For most adverbs with two or more syllables, add **most**.

> EXAMPLES: Of all the guests, Sally left earliest.
> Of all the ice cream sodas, this one tastes most delicious.

POSITIVE	COMPARATIVE	SUPERLATIVE
near	nearer	nearest
deep	deeper	deepest
agreeable	more agreeable	most agreeable
often	more often	most often
promptly	more promptly	most promptly
frequently	more frequently	most frequently

WATCH OUT!

Never use **er** with **more** or **less**.

Never use **est** with **most** or **least**.

Some adverbs change their form when used to make comparisons.

> EXAMPLES: Our team played well.
> Our team played better than the other team.
> Our team played best of all the teams in the league.

POSITIVE	COMPARATIVE	SUPERLATIVE
little	less	least
badly	worse	worst
well	better	best
much	more	most

PRACTICE

Underline the adverb or adverbs in each sentence.

> EXAMPLE: Megan waited eagerly for the rain to stop.
>
> ANSWER: Megan waited <u>eagerly</u> for the rain to stop.

1.   Silvia is wearing a bright blue dress.
2.   I have eaten quite enough chocolate cookies.
3.   Please listen especially carefully to the instructions.
4.   Slowly, the leaves changed their colors.
5.   He is always completely prepared for class.

Underline the adverb or adverbs in each sentence. Tell which word each adverb modifies and what part of speech that word is.

> EXAMPLE: My neighbors have never painted their house.
>
> ANSWER: My neighbors have <u>never</u> painted their house. (painted, verb)

6.   You have too many excuses!
7.   The show was cancelled because too few people bought tickets.
8.   This is not a difficult task.
9.   Our class will never forget this lesson.
10. She finished her work earlier than he did.
11. Robert spoke very well.

Underline the interrogative adverb in each sentence.

> EXAMPLE: Where did you put my coat?   ANSWER: <u>Where</u> did you put my coat?

12. Why is there no school on Monday?
13. When are we going to leave?
14. How is your grandmother feeling?

Underline the adverb in each sentence and identify each one as a positive, comparative, or superlative adverb.

> EXAMPLE: The winner ran faster than his teammates.
>
> ANSWER: The winner ran <u>faster</u> than his teammates. (comparative)

15. They danced most gracefully.
16. The car raced quickly down the road.
17. Stan practices more seriously than Harry.
18. My sister Helen is an unusually smart chess player.
19. The finish line is farther away than I thought.
20. Which of your three brothers runs fastest?

PREPOSITIONS

A preposition is a word that shows the relationship between a noun or a pronoun to some other words in the sentence.

EXAMPLES:

The cat jumped over the chair.
The cat jumped under the chair.
The cat jumped behind the chair.
The cat jumped onto the chair.

The preposition shows the relationship of the noun (cat) to the object of the preposition (chair). See page 31 for more about the object of the preposition.

COMMON PREPOSITIONS INCLUDE:

about	among	beneath	during	like	out	to
above	around	beside	except	near	outside	under
across	at	between	for	of	over	until
after	before	by	from	off	past	up
against	behind	concerning	in	on	since	with
along	below	down	into	upon	through	without

COMPOUND PREPOSITIONS

A compound preposition is a preposition that is made up of more than one word.

EXAMPLES: We sat in front of our house.
He went ahead of the class.

COMMON COMPOUND PREPOSITIONS INCLUDE:

ahead of	in front of
along with	in spite of
aside from	instead of
because of	next to
except for	on account of
in addition to	owing to

PRACTICE

Underline all the prepositions or compound prepositions in the sentences below.

EXAMPLE: The stars are in the sky. ANSWER: The stars are in the sky.

1. Sarah had to leave after dinner.
2. She went along with their decision.
3. Ashley and Megan walked on the seashore for hours.
4. Jane gave me the vegetable recipe in addition to the cake recipe.
5. Before his vacation, Matthew read three books.
6. We spent our day at the fair.
7. The woman on my left smiled at you.
8. In spite of the rain, the party was a success.

CONJUNCTIONS

A conjunction is a word that joins single words or groups of words.

COMMONLY USED CONJUNCTIONS				
and	but	for	or	nor
either	neither	yet	so	so that

COORDINATING CONJUNCTIONS

A coordinating conjunction joins words or group of words that have **equal grammatical weight** in a sentence. When a coordinating conjunction is used **between clauses** (see page 36), a comma precedes the coordinating conjunction.

EXAMPLES: You should study for your test immediately, and finish your homework later.
Andrea hid the prizes, so that the children could hunt for them.
Jesse and Mark went sailing.

CORRELATIVE CONJUNCTIONS

Correlative conjunctions work in pairs to join words or groups of words that have equal grammatical weight in a sentence.

EXAMPLES: Both Billy and Amber went skiing.
Neither a borrower nor a lender be.

COMMON CORRELATIVE CONJUNCTIONS	both...and	neither...nor
	either...or	not only...but also
	just as...so	whether...or

SUBORDINATING CONJUNCTIONS

A subordinating conjunction connects a main (independent) clause to a subordinate (dependent) clause. The subordinate clause cannot stand alone as a sentence because its thought is not completely understood without the main clause. (See page 36 for more on clauses.)

EXAMPLES: You will succeed provided you study.
You can tell ghost stories as soon as the sun sets.

COMMON SUBORDINATING CONJUNCTIONS					
after	as long as	considering (that)	in order that	though	whenever
although	as soon as	if	provided (that)	till	where
as	as though	if only	since	unless	whereas
as far as	because	inasmuch as	so that	until	wherever
as if	before	in case	than	when	while

CONJUNCTIVE ADVERBS

A conjunctive adverb is used to clarify the relationship between clauses of equal grammatical weight in a sentence. When a conjunctive adverb is used between clauses, a semicolon precedes the conjunctive adverb, and a comma follows it.

EXAMPLES: I am sitting in front of a roaring fire; still, I am so cold.
The children built a beautiful sandcastle; then, the waves came and washed it away.
We studied all semester; consequently, we passed all our exams.

COMMON CONJUNCTIVE ADVERBS				
again	equally	however	nevertheless	still
also	further	indeed	nonetheless	then
besides	furthermore	instead	otherwise	therefore
consequently	hence	moreover	similarly	thus

PRACTICE

Underline the conjunction in each sentence and indicate whether it is a coordinating conjunction, correlative conjunction, subordinating conjunction, or a conjunctive adverb.

EXAMPLE: Both Billy and his brother went to college just as their father did.
ANSWER: Both Billy and his brother went to college just as their father did. (correlative conjunction)

1. We will leave as soon as Maria comes downstairs.
2.   I forgot to study for the test; however, I still did well.
3. Today I saw my friend Adam, and we played a game of basketball.
4. We will have fun whether we win or lose.
5. Either you or I will have to make dinner tonight.

Use a conjunction to combine the sentences.

EXAMPLE: Edward wants to go to the movies. Jill wants to go to the store.
ANSWER: Edward wants to go to the movies while Jill wants to go to the store.

6. I burned my hand. I cannot play baseball today.
7. I'm a good swimmer. I've taken swimming lessons for five years.
8. I have a little sister. Dan has a little sister.
9. You cannot play on the team. Your grades are poor.
10. We rested at our campsite. The sun rose over the mountain.

INTERJECTIONS 9

An interjection is a word or phrase that expresses a cry or other exclamatory sound expressing surprise, anger, pleasure, or some other emotion or feeling. An interjection has no grammatical connection to other words in the sentence. Commas follow mild interjections; exclamation points follow stronger interjections.

EXAMPLES: Bravo!
Oh no, I forgot my keys.
Ouch!
Elizabeth! Spit that out!
Stop!
Oh my, it's a hot day.

COMMON INTERJECTIONS		
ah	ha	pow
alas	oh	ugh
cool	oh my	whew
darn	oh no	wow
fantastic	ouch	yikes

WOW!

PRACTICE

Underline each interjection in the following sentences.

EXAMPLE: Wait! You forgot your change.
ANSWER: Wait! You forgot your change.

1. Whew! It is so humid.
2. Nonsense! I don't believe a word of it.
3. Good! We have finally won.
4. Oh no, the rain will cancel our game.
5. Stop! I can't stand it anymore.

10 SUBJECT AND PREDICATE

SIMPLE SUBJECTS AND SIMPLE PREDICATES

A **sentence** is a group of words that expresses a **complete thought**. The words in a sentence must be in an order that makes sense.

The main noun or pronoun in a sentence tells what or whom the sentence is about. The main noun or pronoun is the **simple subject** of the sentence.

The main verb or verb phrase in a sentence expresses the action or state of being of the subject. The main verb or verb phrase is the **simple predicate** of the sentence.

EXAMPLES:

	SIMPLE SUBJECT	SIMPLE PREDICATE
Mary had a little lamb.	Mary	had
The radio was loud.	radio	was
We turned the corner slowly.	We	turned
I am going to the movies.	I	am going

COMPLETE SUBJECTS AND COMPLETE PREDICATES

Every sentence has two parts, the complete subject and the complete predicate. The **complete subject** consists of the simple subject plus all the words that modify it. The **complete predicate** consists of the simple predicate plus all the words that modify it.

EXAMPLES:

	COMPLETE SUBJECT	COMPLETE PREDICATE
The bell rang twelve times.	The bell	rang twelve times
Jackson kicked three field goals.	Jackson	kicked three field goals
The car was stopped for speeding.	The car	was stopped for speeding

Sometimes the subject in an imperative sentence (see page 68) (you) is understood and not stated.

EXAMPLES: Tell me your name.
Start the car.
Pick up the groceries.

COMPOUND SUBJECTS AND COMPOUND PREDICATES

A **compound subject** consists of two or more simple subjects that are joined by a conjunction and share the same verb.

EXAMPLES: Carl and Elizabeth went downtown.
Both the dog and the cat are white.

A **compound predicate** (or compound verb) consists of two or more verbs or verb phrases that are joined by a conjunction and share the same subject.

EXAMPLES: The children swam or ran all day.
The couple glided and danced across the floor.
The students studied and learned all year.

It is possible to have both a compound subject and a compound predicate in a sentence.

EXAMPLE: Tom and Juan acted and sang in the play.

COMPOUND SUBJECT   COMPOUND PREDICATE

PRACTICE

Underline the complete subject and circle the complete predicate of the sentence.

EXAMPLE: The child skipped down the road.   ANSWER: The child (skipped down the road.)

1. The maple tree was twenty feet high.
2. The sun rises every morning.
3. The birds built their nest.
4. We went to the doctor's office.
5. The small child stomped his foot.

Underline the simple subject of the sentence and circle the simple predicate.

EXAMPLE: We have asked for extra help.   ANSWER: We (have asked) for extra help.

6. I eat a snack every afternoon.
7. You knew how much it would cost.
8. The pond froze quickly last winter.
9. They shook the sand off their feet.
10. My little brother has written his name for the first time.

Underline the compound subject.

EXAMPLE: The boys and girls have eaten their lunch.
ANSWER: The boys and girls have eaten their lunch.

11. Either Jill or Dan is going to win the contest.
12. Jim and Helen have learned their lessons.
13. Both Los Angeles and San Francisco were shaken by the earthquake.
14. Jeff and Mariko have grown a lot since last summer.
15. Neither you nor the team will practice today.

Underline the compound predicate of each sentence.

EXAMPLE: The boat pitched and swayed in the wind.
ANSWER: The boat pitched and swayed in the wind.

16. Daniel sneezed and coughed.
17. The boys neither ate nor slept.
18. My father moaned and groaned when his team lost.
19. The students either studied or read in the library.
20. The batter swung and missed the baseball.

11 COMPLEMENTS

A complement is a word or group of words that completes the meaning of a verb.

There are four kinds of complements: **direct objects**, **indirect objects**, **object complements**, and **subject complements**.

DIRECT OBJECTS

Direct objects are nouns, pronouns, or words acting as nouns that answers the question **what** or **whom** after a transitive verb. The direct object performs no action on its own but has an action being performed to it.

EXAMPLES:

	VERB	DIRECT OBJECT
He throws a baseball.	throws	baseball
I like it.	like	it

Direct objects can be plural.

EXAMPLES:

	VERB	DIRECT OBJECT
We see a dog and a cat.	see	a dog and a cat
We see them.	see	them

PRONOUNS USED AS:

SUBJECT ONLY	I	we	she	he	they	who					
OBJECT ONLY	me	us	her	him	them	whom					
SUBJECT OR OBJECT	mine	ours	hers	his	theirs	it	that	which	you	yours

EXAMPLES:

CORRECT	INCORRECT
They saw my friend and me.	They saw my friend and I.
She and I went to the store.	She and me went to the store.
The winners are you and she.	The winners are you and her.

INDIRECT OBJECTS

An indirect object answers the question **to whom, for whom, to what,** or **for what** after a transitive verb. The indirect object always appears between the verb and the direct object. The indirect object is the receiver of the direct object.

EXAMPLES:

	VERB	DIRECT OBJECT	INDIRECT OBJECT
Jeanne gave me the picture.	gave	picture	me
Matt threw Charlie the basketball.	threw	basketball	Charlie

OBJECT COMPLEMENTS

An object complement is a noun, pronoun, or adjective that answers the question what **after a direct object**. It completes the meaning of the direct object by identifying or describing it.

Object complements appear only in sentences with direct objects and action verbs that have the general meaning of **make** or **consider**.

SOME ACTION VERBS					
WITH THE GENERAL MEANING OF MAKE OR CONSIDER					
appoint	render	call	elect	name	
choose	find	prove	vote	think	

EXAMPLES:

	ACTION VERB	DIRECT OBJECT	OBJECT COMPLEMENT
My mother considers my room messy.	considers	room	messy
Kevin named his rabbit Fluffy.	named	rabbit	Fluffy
We call our teacher Mr. Science.	call	teacher	Mr. Science

SUBJECT COMPLEMENTS

A subject complement follows a subject and linking verb and identifies or describes the subject.

There are two kinds of subject complements: predicate nominatives and predicate adjectives.

A **predicate nominative** is a noun or a pronoun that follows a linking verb and points back to the subject to **identify it further**.

EXAMPLES:

	SUBJECT	LINKING VERB	PREDICATE NOMINATIVE
Bruce is a pianist.	Bruce	is	pianist
Today is Tuesday.	today	is	Tuesday
Helen became valedictorian.	Helen	became	valedictorian

A **predicate adjective** is an adjective that follows a linking verb and points back to the subject and **further describes it**.

EXAMPLES:

	SUBJECT	LINKING VERB	PREDICATE ADJECTIVE
I feel very happy.	I	feel	happy
The thunder sounds close.	thunder	sounds	close
The monster was terrifying.	monster	was	terrifying

PRACTICE

Underline the complement or complements in each sentence and identify each one as a direct object, indirect object, object complement, predicate nominative, or predicate adjective.

EXAMPLE: We lost our dog.
ANSWER: We lost our <u>dog</u>. (direct object)

1.   Lucy will bake a cake.
2.   Fulton invented the steamboat.
3.   Barbara will show Ginny her room.
4.   Aki sent Eileen a present.
5.   The class named William team leader.
6.   Your kindness made him happy.
7.   Cynthia finds chemistry fascinating.
8.   Washington became our first president.
9.   Our nation's capital is Washington D.C.
10.   Today's homework seemed easy.
11.   Phil was hungry.
12.   Ron is my brother.
13.   The old man looked grumpy.

A phrase is a group of words that **acts as a part of speech**, such as a noun, verb, adjective, or adverb. A phrase is not a complete sentence; it does not have a subject and a predicate.

A phrase may be used as a noun, verb, adjective, or adverb.

EXAMPLES:

	PART OF SPEECH
Seeing the horror movie scared Maria.	noun
I should have come home earlier.	verb
The baby with the curly hair laughs a lot.	adjective
We like to swim in the pool.	adverb

The main types of phrases are prepositional, appositive, absolute, and verbal phrases. Verbal phrases include participle, gerund, and infinitive phrases.

PREPOSITIONAL PHRASES

A prepositional phrase is a group of words that begins with a preposition (see page 22) and usually ends with a noun or a pronoun (the object of the preposition).

A prepositional phrase functions as an adjective when it modifies a noun or a pronoun. A prepositional phrase functions as an adverb when it modifies a verb, an adjective, or an adverb.

The object of the preposition is the noun or pronoun that ends a prepositional phrase.

EXAMPLES:

	OBJECT OF THE PREPOSITION	ACTS AS	MODIFIES
The oldest man on the block lives there.	block	adjective	man (noun)
Which of the cars is faster?	cars	adjective	which (pronoun)
Harrison lives in the city.	city	adverb	lives (verb)
The parents are proud of their son's decision.	decision	adverb	proud (adjective)
The book on the table is mine.	table	adjective	book (noun)
They worked quietly with us yesterday.	us	adverb	quietly (adverb)

Prepositional phrases may occur in series of two or more and may have more than one object.

EXAMPLES: The treasure was found on the island under the palm tree.

TWO PREPOSITIONAL PHRASES

The book was about love, honor, and commitment.

THREE OBJECTS OF THE PREPOSITION

APPOSITIVES AND APPOSITIVE PHRASES

An **appositive** is a noun or a pronoun that is placed next to another noun or pronoun to identify it or give additional information about it.

EXAMPLE:

	APPOSITIVE
My friend Paula is a whiz on the computer.	identifies the noun friend

An **appositive phrase** is an appositive plus any words that modify the appositive. Use commas to set off any appositive or appositive phrases that are not necessary to the meaning of the sentence.

EXAMPLES:

	APPOSITIVE PHRASE
Irene, a great beauty, always lit up the room.	identifies Irene
Carl traveled with Tom, a childhood friend, to Boston.	gives information about Tom

VERBALS AND VERBAL PHRASES

A **verbal** is a verb form that functions in a sentence as a **noun**, an **adjective**, or an **adverb**. A verbal never functions as a verb. Verbals are **participles**, **gerunds**, and **infinitives**.

A **verbal phrase** is a verbal and any complements and modifiers.

PARTICIPLES AND PARTICIPIAL PHRASES

A participle is a verb form that can function as an **adjective**. **Present participles** always end in **ing**. **Past participles** often end in **ed**. Many common adjectives are participles.

EXAMPLES:

They left the sinking ship.	present participle
The scribbled note was unreadable.	past participle
The lost boy missed his mother.	past participle

A **participial phrase** contains a participle and any complements and modifiers. Participial phrases always act as **adjectives** and can be in the present or past tense. Use commas to set off any participial phrases that are not necessary to the meaning of the sentence.

EXAMPLES:

The picture hanging on the wall looks like a Picasso.
Having been burned once, I am very careful near fires.
Tim, swimming his best, won the race.
Looking for peace and quiet, I found a lovely garden.

A **past participle** can sometimes be used with the present participle of the auxiliary (or helping) verbs **have** or **be**.

EXAMPLES: Having seen the dolphins swim, I wanted to swim with them.
Being lost and tired, Anna asked for directions.

GERUNDS AND GERUND PHRASES

A **gerund** is a verb form that ends in **ing** and is used as a noun.

EXAMPLES: Carl loves sailing.
Cooking is Laura's passion.

A **gerund phrase** contains a gerund and any complements and modifiers.

EXAMPLES: Walking to the store took fifteen minutes.
Jumping high is the object of this contest.
Working all day makes Jack a dull boy.

Do not confuse a gerund with a present participle, which also ends with **ing** but is used as an adjective.

EXAMPLES: The ticking clock was annoying.   (Ticking is a present participle.)
The ticking of the clock was annoying.   (Ticking is a gerund.)
Ticking away, the clock was annoying.   (Ticking away is a gerund phrase.)

INFINITIVES AND INFINITIVE PHRASES

An **infinitive** is a verb form that is usually preceded by the word **to**, and is used as a **noun**, an **adjective**, or an **adverb**.

EXAMPLES:

	FUNCTIONS AS
Joseph wants to stay.	noun
The child felt the urge to jump.	adjective
Everyone is prepared to eat.	adverb

An **infinitive phrase** contains an infinitive and any complements and modifiers. An infinitive phrase can be used as a **noun**, an **adjective**, or an **adverb** and is usually preceded by the word **to**.

EXAMPLES:

	FUNCTIONS AS
To prepare thoroughly is always a good idea.	noun
That would be a good museum to visit next week.	adjective
Tracy was waiting to board the train.	adverb

ABSOLUTE PHRASES

An **absolute phrase** (or a nominative absolute) consists of a noun or a pronoun that is modified by a participle or a participial phrase. An absolute phrase has no grammatical relation to the rest of the sentence. In some absolute phrases, the participle **being** is understood rather than stated.

EXAMPLES: We arrived early, the roads having little traffic.
With the stars (being) so bright, it was a perfect night to study the constellations.

PRACTICE

Identify the function (noun, verb, adjective, or adverb) of each underlined phrase.

EXAMPLE: The man ran <u>on the track</u>. ANSWER: (adverb)

1. <u>Playing in the park</u> is my favorite pastime.
2. I can be there <u>at eight o'clock</u>.
3. The woman <u>in the red dress</u> is very pretty.
4. We <u>couldn't have left</u> school any sooner.
5. The car <u>in the garage</u> is blue.
6. Brian likes <u>to read mysteries</u>.
7. I <u>must not have been</u> the only one absent.
8. Jean danced <u>with Jim</u>.
9. The equipment <u>inside the locker</u> was very valuable.
10. <u>To see the new house</u> will be fun.

Underline the prepositional phrase in each of the following sentences.

EXAMPLE: Dinner is on the table. ANSWER: Dinner is <u>on the table</u>.

11. The star fell from the sky.
12. The school was around the corner.
13. During recess we sell milk and cookies.
14. The trapeze artist performed without a net.
15. The ship was lost beneath the sea.

Underline the participial phrase in each of the following sentences.

EXAMPLE: Mary, dressed in her Halloween costume, went to the party.
ANSWER: Mary, <u>dressed in her Halloween costume</u>, went to the party.

16. Many immigrants came to America hoping to make their fortunes.
17. Demonstrating ingenuity, the boys sold lemonade on the corner.
18. Looking through my field glasses, I watched the batter strike out.
19. The flowers growing in the park were quite colorful.
20. The car came around the corner, trying to make the light.

Combine the following sentences by making the second sentence into an appositive or appositive phrase.

EXAMPLE: Brian just won first prize in the science fair. Brian is my brother.
ANSWER: Brian, my brother, just won first prize in the science fair.

21. Donna is a straight A student. Donna is a classmate.

22. My birthday is in June. June is a summer month.

23. San Diego has nice beaches. San Diego is my hometown.

24. My brother can be really annoying. Mark is my brother.

Change each sentence so that it begins with a gerund or a gerund phrase.

EXAMPLE: My hobby is to collect stamps.
ANSWER: Collecting stamps is my hobby.

25. Daily exercise is a good habit.

26. To play video games is fun.

27. To see a rainbow is exhilarating.

28. To swim laps is relaxing.

Underline the infinitive or infinitive phrase in each sentence.

EXAMPLE: Elizabeth wanted to take a nap.
ANSWER: Elizabeth wanted to take a nap.

29. The dog started to growl fiercely.

30. They had the desire to dance.

31. She was delighted to have won.

32. To learn this material will not be difficult.

33. They chose to live in the suburbs.

Combine the following sentences by making the second sentence into an absolute phrase.

EXAMPLE: Today I am going to Annapolis. Annapolis is the capital of Maryland.
ANSWER: Today I am going to Annapolis, the capital of Maryland.

34. The team took a break. The task was completed.

35. We had a great party. We planned the activities in advance.

36. He missed the train. He woke up late.

37. The garden is more fragrant than ever. The lilacs are in bloom along the pathway.

38. She wrote her term paper on Asia. She hopes to visit Asia one day.

CLAUSES

A clause is a group of words that has a subject and a predicate, and functions as a part of a sentence.

A **main clause** (or independent clause) has a subject and a predicate, and can stand alone as a sentence.

A **subordinate clause** (or dependent clause) has a subject and a predicate, but cannot stand alone as a complete sentence. A subordinate clause enhances the thought expressed in the main clause.

> EXAMPLE: Their rooms were messy until they decided to clean them.
>
>   MAIN CLAUSE   SUBORDINATE CLAUSE

A subordinate clause usually begins with a subordinating conjunction (see page 23).

There are three types of subordinate clauses: **adjective clauses**, **adverb clauses**, and **noun clauses**.

ADJECTIVE CLAUSES

An adjective clause is a subordinate clause that modifies a **noun** or a **pronoun** and usually comes after the word it modifies. An adjective clause may begin with a relative pronoun (see page 9) or **where** or **when**.

> EXAMPLES: A person who values his money will not squander it.
>   The cake that I made for your birthday is chocolate with chocolate icing.

An adjective clause may be an essential (or restrictive) clause or a nonessential (or nonrestrictive) clause.

An **essential clause** is an adjective clause that is needed to make the meaning of the sentence clear. A clause starting with **that** is an essential clause. This type of clause is never set off with commas.

> EXAMPLES: The actor who won the award could not remember his speech.
>   The photo that won first prize was Charlie's.
>   The dog that barked all night is my cousin's.

A **nonessential clause** is an adjective clause that is not needed to make the meaning of the sentence clear. A clause starting with **which** is a nonessential clause. This type of clause is always set off with commas.

> EXAMPLES: Patrick, who was in trouble often, was the class clown.
>   We took a trip to the museum, which was enjoyable.

ADVERB CLAUSES

An **adverb clause** is a subordinate clause that modifies a verb, an adjective, or an adverb. It tells **when**, **where**, **why**, **how**, **to what extent,** or **under what condition**. An adverb clause is usually introduced by a subordinating conjunction (see page 23).

> EXAMPLE: The fire drill started when the alarm rang.

When an adverb clause comes before the main clause, separate it from the main clause with a comma.

> EXAMPLE: When the alarm rang, the fire drill started.

Elliptical adverb clauses have words left out of them in order to avoid repetition and awkwardness. The omitted words are implied or easily understood by the reader.

> EXAMPLE: When (I am) in the garden, I try to take time to smell the roses.

NOUN CLAUSES

A **noun clause** is a subordinate clause that is used as a noun. A noun clause can be used as if it were a noun or a pronoun: as a subject, a direct object, an indirect object, an object of a preposition, or a predicate nominative.

EXAMPLES:

	USED AS
Whatever gift you give will be appreciated.	subject
The artist demonstrated how the paint was mixed.	direct object
She gave whoever came early a new book.	indirect object
The cat jumps on whomever it likes.	object of the preposition
A good saying is a penny saved is a penny earned.	predicate nominative

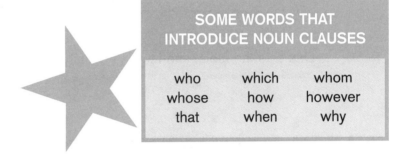

SOME WORDS THAT INTRODUCE NOUN CLAUSES

who	which	whom
whose	how	however
that	when	why

PRACTICE

Underline the subordinate clause in each sentence and identify it as an adjective clause, adverb clause, or noun clause.

EXAMPLE: When I don't get enough sleep, I get cranky.
ANSWER: <u>When I don't get enough sleep</u>, I get cranky. (adverb clause)

1. Even though it was late, we did not feel tired.
2. The computer that I used today is in the library.
3. I will interview whichever person runs for office.
4. This is the spot where I lost my watch.
5. The team left the field after the sun went down.
6. This is the woman who picked the winning lottery number.
7. The man who painted our house is a relative of yours.
8. He will not show me what he painted.
9. As soon as you are ready, the test will begin.
10. The Statue of Liberty, which I saw last month, is one of my favorite tourist attractions.
11. He was instructed to begin when the clock struck two.
12. I did not know that Pike's Peak is in Colorado.
13. Wherever you go, our best wishes will be with you.

SENTENCE STRUCTURE

SIMPLE SENTENCES

A simple sentence has only **one complete subject** and **one complete predicate**.

EXAMPLES: The little boy ate a sandwich.

COMPLETE SUBJECT · COMPLETE PREDICATE

COMPOUND SENTENCES

A compound sentence contains **two or more main clauses**. They are joined by either a comma followed by a conjunction, by a semicolon alone, or by a semicolon and a conjunctive adverb.

A conjunction is a word that is used to connect words or groups of words (see pages 23-24).

EXAMPLES: I like to go to school, but I enjoy my days off.

MAIN CLAUSE · MAIN CLAUSE

Dan sets the table, and his sister washes the dishes.

MAIN CLAUSE · MAIN CLAUSE

COMPLEX SENTENCES

A complex sentence has **one main clause** and **one or more subordinate clauses**.

EXAMPLES: Although we like Japanese food, we went to a Mexican restaurant.

SUBORDINATE CLAUSE · MAIN CLAUSE

I went to the store after leaving home.

MAIN CLAUSE · SUBORDINATE CLAUSE

COMPOUND-COMPLEX SENTENCES

A compound-complex sentence has **two or more main clauses** and **one or more subordinate clauses**.

EXAMPLES: George was gardening, and when the sprinkler came on, he got soaked.

MAIN CLAUSE · SUBORDINATE CLAUSE · MAIN CLAUSE

Sally, who is a very busy woman, teaches three classes each day and conducts the orchestra.

SUBORDINATE CLAUSE · MAIN CLAUSE · MAIN CLAUSE

SENTENCE FRAGMENTS

A sentence fragment is punctuated as though it were a complete sentence, but it is missing a subject, a verb, or both.

EXAMPLES:

		WHAT'S MISSING?
FRAGMENT:	Bought a sweater.	subject
COMPLETE:	My aunt bought a sweater.	
FRAGMENT:	You the boss.	verb
COMPLETE:	You are the boss.	
FRAGMENT:	At my house.	subject *and* verb
COMPLETE:	We will meet at my house.	

RUN-ON SENTENCES

A run-on sentence is two or more clauses written as one sentence. You can correct a run-on sentence by writing each clause as a complete sentence, joining the clauses with a semicolon, or joining the clauses with a comma and a conjunction.

RUN-ON SENTENCE: Aja was promoted to manager she is very reliable.
EXAMPLES WRITTEN CORRECTLY: Aja was promoted to manager. She is very reliable.
Aja was promoted to manager; she is very reliable.
Aja was promoted to manager, and she is very reliable.

PRACTICE

Use a comma and a conjunction to make each pair of sentences into a compound sentence.

EXAMPLE: The bell rang. The class was not dismissed.
ANSWER: The bell rang, but the class was not dismissed.

1.   Do you want to go out? Shall we stay home?

2.   Tom and I laughed. Nobody else thought the joke was funny.

3.   She asked Jim and me to join her. We had other plans.

4.   Those keys are mine. These keys are yours.

5.   Jim went to the dentist. His mother waited in the car.

Rewrite each run-on sentence as two sentences using correct punctuation marks.

EXAMPLE: Was the television turned off all the children were reading.

ANSWER: Was the television turned off? All the children were reading.

6. We drove back from our trip last night the ride took two hours.

_____

7. Whose team will they play next you and he bought tickets.

_____

8. You and I will bring them to the park will their mother be there.

_____

9. I looked for you at the store we ate lunch without you.

_____

10. What time did you come home I came home very early.

_____

Underline the main clauses and circle the subordinate clauses. Indicate whether the sentence is a compound sentence, a complex sentence, or a compound-complex sentence.

EXAMPLE: The car stopped when it ran out of gas.

ANSWER: The car stopped (when it ran out of gas.) (complex)

11. She told a funny joke, and we all laughed.

12. The girls did not arrive on time but, because we knew they were coming, we prepared dinner.

13. If it keeps snowing, I will build a snowman and my friends will build an igloo.

14. Although it is sunny, it is not warm.

15. Will you stay, or will you go?

16. The party ended when the clock struck twelve, and all the guests went home.

17. I thought it was the right answer, but the teacher marked it incorrect.

18. Although I am afraid of heights, I went to the top of the Empire State Building and, to my surprise, I enjoyed the view.

19. While you are up, please answer the phone.

20. I must see the giraffes whenever I go to the zoo.

21. Bernie visited with me while you were on vacation but she didn't stay long enough.

15

All verbs have four principal parts: a **base form**, a **present participle**, a **simple past form**, and a **past participle**. All verb tenses are formed from these principal parts.

BASE FORM	PRESENT PARTICIPLE	PAST FORM	PAST PARTICIPLE
be	being	was, were	been
play	playing	played	played
speak	speaking	spoke	spoken

The **past participle of a regular verb** is formed by adding **ed** or **d** to the base form and must always be preceeded by one or more auxiliary verbs.

BASE FORM	PAST FORM	PAST PARTICIPLE
jump	jumped	jumped
type	typed	typed
smell	smelled	smelled
close	closed	closed

The spelling of some **regular verbs** changes when you add **ed**.

BASE FORM	PAST FORM	PAST PARTICIPLE
stop	stopped	stopped
cry	cried	cried
plan	planned	planned

For irregular verbs, the **past form** and **past participle** are formed in ways other than by adding **ed** or **d** to the base form.

BASE FORM	PAST FORM	PAST PARTICIPLE
be, am, are, is	was, were	been
become	became	become
fly	flew	flown
lay	laid	laid
throw	threw	thrown
write	wrote	written

PRACTICE

Form the present participle, past form, and past participle of the verbs listed below.

		PRESENT PARTICIPLE	PAST FORM	PAST PARTICIPLE
EXAMPLE:	laugh	laughing	laughed	laughed
1.	walk	_____	_____	_____
2.	fall	_____	_____	_____
3.	put	_____	_____	_____
4.	run	_____	_____	_____
5.	work	_____	_____	_____

Form the past form and past participle of the irregular verbs listed below.

		PAST FORM	PAST PARTICIPLE
EXAMPLE:	draw	drew	drawn
6.	lead	_____	_____
7.	know	_____	_____
8.	choose	_____	_____
9.	freeze	_____	_____
10.	grow	_____	_____
11.	shake	_____	_____
12.	swing	_____	_____
13.	tear	_____	_____
14.	shine	_____	_____
15.	bring	_____	_____
16.	drink	_____	_____
17.	forget	_____	_____
18.	go	_____	_____
19.	lend	_____	_____
20.	lie	_____	_____
21.	run	_____	_____
22.	ride	_____	_____
23.	ring	_____	_____
24.	speed	_____	_____
25.	swim	_____	_____
26.	take	_____	_____

The tense of a verb indicates its **time**.

There are six tenses: **present**, **past**, **future**, **present perfect**, **past perfect**, and **future perfect**.

PRESENT TENSE

The present tense of the verb expresses a constant, repeated, or habitual action or condition. It can also express a general truth.

EXAMPLES:

Every morning I drink coffee.	habitual
The Mississippi River flows into the Gulf of Mexico.	constant
Water runs down hill.	general truth

The present tense of the verb (except the verb be) is the same as the verb's base form, except for the third person singular where you add **s** or **es**.

★ REMINDER

First person refers to the speaker.
Second person refers to the person spoken to.
Third person refers to the person or thing spoken about.

For more on person and how it affects pronouns see page 7.

PRESENT TENSE

THE VERB be

	SINGULAR	PLURAL
FIRST PERSON	I **am** short.	We **are** short.
SECOND PERSON	You **are** short.	You **are** short.
THIRD PERSON	He/she/it **is** short.	They **are** short.

THE VERB sing

	SINGULAR	PLURAL
FIRST PERSON	I **sing**.	We **sing**.
SECOND PERSON	You **sing**.	You **sing**.
THIRD PERSON	He/she/it **sings**.	They **sing**.

PAST TENSE

The past tense expresses an action or a condition that was **started and completed** in the past.

The past tense is formed by adding **ed** to the base form. The verb **be** has two past tense forms, **was** and **were**.

PAST TENSE		
THE VERB be		
	SINGULAR	PLURAL
FIRST PERSON	I **was** cold.	We **were** cold.
SECOND PERSON	You **were** cold.	You **were** cold.
THIRD PERSON	He/she/it **was** cold.	They **were** cold.
THE VERB walk		
	SINGULAR	PLURAL
FIRST PERSON	I **walked** to school.	We **walked** to school.
SECOND PERSON	You **walked** to school.	You **walked** to school.
THIRD PERSON	He/she/it **walked** to school.	They **walked** to school.

FUTURE TENSE

The future tense expresses an action or a condition that will occur **in the future**.

The future tense is formed by using the auxiliary verb **shall** or **will** with the base form of the verb.

> EXAMPLES: I will make my own Halloween costume.
> Amber will play basketball tomorrow.
> Carl will build a bookshelf.
> Shall we go to the store now?

You can also form the future tense by using the words **going to** or **is about to** with the present tense of the verb **be** and the **base form** of a verb.

> EXAMPLES: My mother is going to bake today.
> My brother is about to make a presentation.

Another way to form the future tense is to use the present tense with an adverb or an adverb phrase that shows future time.

> EXAMPLES: Carl plants flowers in the summer.
> The concert comes to town next month.

PERFECT TENSES

Present Perfect Tense

> The present perfect tense expresses an action or a condition that occurred at some indefinite time in the past, or that began in the past and continues into the present.
>
> The present perfect tense is formed by using **has** or **have** with the **past participle** of a verb.
>
> EXAMPLES: Megan has written a book.
> Michael and Sean have seen this movie.
> It seems as though he has been here forever!

Past Perfect Tense

> The past perfect tense indicates that one past action or condition **began and ended** before another past action or condition started.
>
> The past perfect tense is formed by using the auxiliary verb **had** with the **past participle** of a verb.
>
> EXAMPLE: We had rehearsed the play many times before we opened the show.
>
> PAST PERFECT TENSE . PAST TENSE

Future Perfect Tense

> The future perfect tense expresses one future action or condition that **will begin and end** before another future event starts.
>
> The future tense is formed by using **will have** or **shall have** with the **past participle** of a verb.
>
> EXAMPLE: By the time vacation is over, I will have read ten books.

PROGRESSIVE FORMS

Each of the six tenses has a progressive form that expresses continuing action.

For the progressive form, use the appropriate tense of the verb **be** with the **present participle** of the main verb.

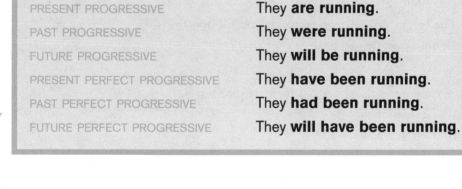

PROGRESSIVE FORMS	
PRESENT PROGRESSIVE	They **are running**.
PAST PROGRESSIVE	They **were running**.
FUTURE PROGRESSIVE	They **will be running**.
PRESENT PERFECT PROGRESSIVE	They **have been running**.
PAST PERFECT PROGRESSIVE	They **had been running**.
FUTURE PERFECT PROGRESSIVE	They **will have been running**.

EMPHATIC FORMS

The present and past tenses have additional forms called **emphatic** that add special force or emphasis to the verb.

For the emphatic form, use **do**, **does**, or **did** with the base form of the verb.

EXAMPLES: You do bake delicious cookies.   present emphatic
Charlie does throw a fast baseball.   present emphatic
We did eat a large meal on Thanksgiving.   past emphatic

COMPATIBILITY OF VERB TENSES

When two or more events occur at the same time, the verbs must be in the same tense.

INCORRECT: The football team scored a touchdown, and the crowd cheers.
CORRECT: The football team scored a touchdown, and the crowd cheered.

When one event precedes or follows the other event, the shifting of tenses is required to show the time difference.

INCORRECT: By the time the boat sailed, the tide changed.
CORRECT: By the time the boat sailed, the tide had changed.

PRACTICE

Underline the correct present tense form of the verb.

EXAMPLE: He visit/visits his grandmother every Sunday.
ANSWER: He visits his grandmother every Sunday.

1.   They move/moves the furniture every few months.
2.   The family plan/plans a long vacation.
3.   Pierina love/loves her little brother.
4.   The bright girl answer/answers difficult questions.
5.   Dennis learn/learns basic social studies.

Change each underlined verb to form its past tense.

EXAMPLE: He opens the car door.   ANSWER: He opened the car door.

6.   Mark bounces the ball.
7.   I am happy.
8.   Shane and Connor like those cookies.
9.   Mike plays with his new puppy.
10.   Diane walks all the way home.

Change each underlined verb to its future tense.

EXAMPLE: We <u>looked</u> for seashells on the beach.
ANSWER: We <u>will look</u> for seashells on the beach.

11. She <u>turns</u> the pages for the pianist at the concert.
12. The mother <u>baked</u> chocolate cookies for the children.
13. We <u>used</u> new art supplies for the project.
14. My best friend <u>bought</u> tickets for both of us.
15. I <u>worked</u> on my report this weekend.

In each of the following sentences, change the verb to the present perfect tense.

EXAMPLE: I visited with my aunt.   ANSWER: I <u>have visited</u> with my aunt.

16. The girls saw this movie.
17. She talked for two hours.
18. Jennifer jumped rope.
19. My parents drove to Canada.
20. Tim drew the colorful pictures.

Identify the tense of each underlined verb as present, past, or future.

EXAMPLE: Alice <u>looked</u> through the looking glass.   ANSWER: past tense

21. My neighbor's dog <u>barked</u> all night long.
22. I <u>shall explain</u> the lesson again.
23. Silvia <u>works</u> very hard on her papers.
24. Albert, please <u>shut</u> the door now.
25. The lecturer <u>talked</u> for nearly two hours.

Underline the correct form of the verb in each sentence.

EXAMPLE: Venita washes/washed the dishes last night.
ANSWER: Venita <u>washed</u> the dishes last night.

26. The flowers bloomed/bloom last June.
27. Manny, please walk/walks to the store right now.
28. No one stand/stands on the stage.
29. The high school team play/plays football every year.
30. Yesterday, Louisa recites/recited her piece very well.

Underline and identify the present perfect tense verb, the past perfect tense verb, or the future perfect tense verb in each sentence below.

EXAMPLE: By noon, Steve will have gone home.
ANSWER: By noon, Steve will have gone home. (future perfect tense)

31. As of April fifteenth, she will have worked here one year.

32. Abe has gone to the store.

33. She had studied Latin before she took French.

34. The game will have started by the time we get there.

35. Before the restoration began, Mr. Jones had bought the house.

36. Maria will have planted all the flowers before I get back.

37. Ben and Jerry have made a mess.

38. By tomorrow you will have sailed to the island.

39. He told me what I had told you earlier.

40. After this hike, David will have walked ten miles.

Using each of the following verbs, write a sentence with the verb in the emphatic form.

EXAMPLE: enjoy
ANSWER: I do enjoy painting.

41. grow _____

42. ride _____

43. smile _____

44. play _____

45. sleep _____

Rewrite the following sentences so that the tense of the second verb agrees with the tense of the first verb.

EXAMPLE: I am studying French because I had an exam next week.
ANSWER: I am studying French because I have an exam next week.

46. The band played loudly, and the couples dance.

47. The comedian telling funny jokes makes the audience laughed.

48. The sun set over the hills before the rain falls.

49. When I get hungry, I had a snack.

50. John crossed the finish line first, and his coach cheers.

VOICE OF VERBS

Voice is the property of a verb that shows whether the subject acts or is acted upon. An action verb can be used in the **active** voice or in the **passive** voice.

A verb is in the **active** voice when the subject performs the action. If the sentence has a direct object, the verb is in the active voice.

EXAMPLES: Nathalie climbed the tallest tree.
Our team won the race.
The boys built a model airplane.

A verb is in the **passive** voice when its action is performed on the subject. The passive voice is formed by using the past participle of a verb with a form of the verb **be**.

EXAMPLES: The tallest tree was climbed by Nathalie.
The race was won by our team.
A model airplane was built by the boys.

MOOD OF VERBS

Mood is the property of a verb that shows the manner in which the action or condition is expressed. A verb express one of three moods: the **indicative** mood, the **imperative** mood, or the **subjunctive** mood.

The **indicative** mood makes a statement or asks a question.

EXAMPLES: Have you finished your project yet?
Carol went home.
We had a wonderful vacation.

The **imperative** mood expresses a command or makes a request.

EXAMPLES: Don't jaywalk.
Please wash the dishes.
Do your homework before watching television.

Subjunctive mood expresses indirectly a demand, recommendation, suggestion, or statement of necessity.

EXAMPLES: I suggest that you study for the test.
It is important to eat breakfast daily.
It is good to be prepared.

The subjunctive mood may also be used to state a condition or a wish that is contrary to fact. This use always requires the past tense and often follows the word **if**.

EXAMPLES: I wish I could play the piano.
If I had a nickel for every time I heard that, I'd be a millionaire.
If wishes were horses, I would have a stable.

PRACTICE

Underline the verb in each sentence and tell whether it is in the active or passive voice.

EXAMPLE: The train moved slowly.

ANSWER: The train <u>moved</u> slowly. (active voice)

1. The teenager watched the teacher.
2. The glass was broken.
3. Jennifer finished third in the race.
4. The children rode the pony all afternoon.
5. The tent was pitched by the scout leader.
6. The race was won by our team.
7. Mary sang in the choir.
8. They caught the bus to the store.
9. The garden was planted by Mike.
10. The dinner was prepared by Sheila.

Underline the verb in each sentence and tell whether it is in the indicative, imperative, or subjunctive mood.

EXAMPLE: Turn the music down.

ANSWER: <u>Turn</u> the music down. (imperative mood)

11. Please clean your room.
12. Joseph got an A on his exam.
13. May the better player win.
14. Keep an eye on the dog.
15. The trip to the zoo was fun.
16. I recommend that you arrive early.
17. Did you see that?
18. Study for your test.
19. My canary sings sweetly.
20. It would be wise to pack lightly.

SUBJECT AND VERB AGREEMENT

A verb must agree with its subject in **person** and **number**. See chapter 16 for more on person. Number indicates if a word is singular or plural. A singular subject indicates one and requires a singular verb. A plural subject indicates more than one and requires a plural verb. To form a singular verb add **s** or **es** to a regular verb.

EXAMPLES:

SINGULAR	SUBJECT	VERB	PLURAL	SUBJECT	VERB
The artist paints.	artist	paints	The artists paint.	artists	paint
The owl screeches.	owl	screeches	The owls screech.	owls	screech

In verb phrases, the auxiliary (or helping) verbs **be**, **have**, and **do** change form to show agreement with third person subjects. These auxiliary verbs change form while the main verbs do not.

EXAMPLES:

SINGULAR	PLURAL
I am tired.	We are tired.
She is dancing.	They are dancing.
It has slid down.	They have slid down.
Does that look red?	Do those look red?

INVERTED SENTENCES

Inverted sentences are sentences where the **subject follows the verb**. The inverted sentence often begins with a prepositional phrase followed by the verb and then the subject. Remember, the verb must agree with the subject, not the prepositional phrase.

EXAMPLES:

SINGULAR	PLURAL
Above the desk is the diploma.	Above the desk are the diplomas.

In sentences that begin with **there** or **here**, the subject will follow the verb. (Rarely is the word there or here used as the subject of a sentence.)

EXAMPLES:

SINGULAR	PLURAL
Here is the pen.	Here are the pens.
There is the car.	There are the cars.

Questions are inverted sentences. The subject of the sentence is usually found between the auxiliary (or helping) verb and the main verb.

EXAMPLES:

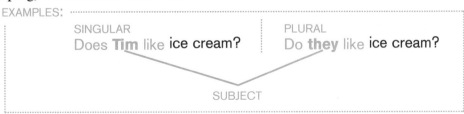

SINGULAR	PLURAL
Does **Tim** like ice cream?	Do **they** like ice cream?

SUBJECT

COMPOUND SUBJECTS

A compound subject consists of two or more subjects in a sentence that share a verb. A compound subject that is joined by **and** or **both… and** is plural and takes a plural verb. A compound subject having two parts that make up one unit takes a singular verb.

SINGULAR EXAMPLE: Macaroni and cheese is tasty to eat.

COMPOUND SUBJECT (ONE UNIT)   SINGULAR VERB

PLURAL EXAMPLE: Both Carlos and Michael are trying out for the team.

COMPOUND SUBJECT (PLURAL)   PLURAL VERB

Compound subjects joined by **or**, **nor**, **either… or**, **neither… nor** must have the verb agree with the subject closer to it.

SINGULAR EXAMPLE: Either Jack or Jill **sings** in the choir.
PLURAL EXAMPLE: Neither the director nor the actors **like** the theater.

A compound subject that starts with **many a**, **every**, or **each** takes a singular verb.

EXAMPLE: Every Tom, Dick, and Harry **likes** sports.

COLLECTIVE NOUNS

A collective noun names a **group** of persons, things, or animals. A collective noun is singular when it refers to a group as a whole; it requires a singular verb. A collective noun is plural when it refers to members of a group as individuals; it requires a plural verb.

SINGULAR EXAMPLE: The band plays at the concert.
PLURAL EXAMPLE: The band play different instruments.

INTERVENING PHRASES AND CLAUSES

The verb must agree with the subject of the sentence not the object in a prepositional phrase.

EXAMPLES: The scent from all the flowers is overwhelming.
Harry, with his younger brothers, is going to the library.

SPECIAL NOUNS

Certain nouns ending in **s** such as mathematics, mumps, and news take singular verbs. Certain other nouns ending in **s** such as scissors, pants, and eyeglasses take plural verbs.

SINGULAR EXAMPLE: The hometown news releases local interest stories.
PLURAL EXAMPLE: His pants look wrinkled.

NOUNS OF AMOUNT

When a noun of amount or quantity refers to a single unit, it requires a singular verb. When a noun of amount or quantity refers to several individual units, it requires a plural verb.

SINGULAR EXAMPLE: Fifteen percent of the bill is a customary tip.

PLURAL EXAMPLE: There are twelve dollars in my wallet.

PHRASES AND CLAUSES AS THE SUBJECT

When a phrase or a clause acts as the subject of the sentence, the verb is always singular.

EXAMPLES:

	SINGULAR VERB
Whoever reaches the finish line first wins the race.	wins
Skating on the lake is lots of fun.	is
To study daily is a good habit.	is

PRACTICE

Underline the verb that is in agreement with the subject.

EXAMPLE: Erin want/wants to go to the movies.   ANSWER: Erin wants to go to the movies.

1.   Ham and eggs is/are my favorite breakfast.
2.   Mark and Alan is/are going to the movies.
3.   Neither my brother nor sister is/are home.
4.   His pants is/are blue.
5.   Neither the team nor the coach like/likes to play in the rain.
6.   Andrea, along with the other flutists, hope/hopes to qualify for the contest.
7.   The family go/goes on a picnic.
8.   Jack, Tim, and Bob receive/receives their allowance every Monday.
9.   Four hours is/ are too long to wait on line.
10. Fifteen dollars is/are the price of the shirt.
11. Half of the tickets was/were sold.
12. Attaining good grades show/shows that you learned your lessons.
13. Tom's paintings are the most beautiful that have/has been displayed.
14. Social studies is/are the subject scheduled for the first period.
15. The bunch of bananas is/are hanging from the tree.

19 MODIFYING CORRECTLY

GOOD, WELL, BAD, BADLY

Good is always used as an **adjective**. **Well** is used as an **adverb** telling how something is done, or as an adjective meaning "in good health." The correct answer to the question, "How are you doing?" is "I am well," not, "I am good."

> EXAMPLES: The Yankees played a good game.
> How well Helen sings!
> Sonia is feeling well.

Bad is always an **adjective** and is used after a being or linking verb. **Badly** is an **adverb** and follows an action verb.

> EXAMPLES: My cousin is a very bad singer.
> We had a bad phone connection.
> I feel bad today.
> The team played badly this afternoon.
> I slept badly last night.
> That boy reacted badly when he heard that he had lost.

DOUBLE NEGATIVES

Two negative words in the same sentence form a double negative. The two negatives cancel each other out. In English, never use a double negative in a sentence.

Use only **one negative** in a sentence to express a negative idea.

NEGATIVES INCLUDE:					POSITIVE FORMS INCLUDE:
no	none	nobody	nowhere	hardly	either
not	nothing	never	neither	scarcely	every
NEGATIVE CONTRACTIONS INCLUDE:					any
can't	isn't	hasn't	wouldn't		anybody
wasn't	didn't	couldn't	shouldn't		anyone
see page 73 for more on contractions					anything
					anywhere

> INCORRECT: You can't take nobody with you.
> CORRECT: You can't take anybody with you.
> INCORRECT: I don't need no help.
> CORRECT: I don't need any help.

DANGLING OR MISPLACED MODIFIERS

Misplaced modifiers modify the wrong word or seem to modify more than one word in a sentence. You may correct a sentence with a misplaced modifier by moving the modifier as close as possible to the word it modifies.

MISPLACED: He saw a squirrel attack the bird feeder reading the Sunday paper.
(Was the bird feeder reading the Sunday paper?)

CORRECT: While reading the Sunday paper, he saw a squirrel attack the bird feeder.

MISPLACED: Moving rapidly we saw the canoe as it raced down the river.
(Were we moving rapidly, or was the canoe moving rapidly?)

CORRECT: We saw the canoe moving rapidly as it raced down the river.

Dangling modifiers can appear to modify no word at all in a sentence. You may correct a sentence that has a dangling modifier by supplying the word it should modify.

DANGLING: Using a telescope, the flying saucer was seen.
(This sentence needs a word that tells who was using a telescope.)

CORRECT: Using a telescope, the astronomer saw the flying saucer.

DANGLING: Working all weekend, the science project was completed.
(Who was working all weekend? The phrase working all weekend modifies no word in the sentence.)

CORRECT: Working all weekend, I completed the science project.

The adverb **only** needs to be placed immediately before the word or group of words that it modifies, or the meaning of the sentence is unclear.

INCORRECT: Tom only goes to the movies on Saturday.
(Does Tom only go to the movies and nowhere else on Saturday, or is Saturday the only day of the week that he goes to the movies?)

CORRECT: Tom goes to the movies only on Saturday.
(Saturday is the only day Tom goes to the movies.)

OR: Tom goes only to the movies on Saturday.
(On Saturday, the only place Tom goes is to the movies.)

PRACTICE

Underline the correct adverb in each sentence.

EXAMPLE: Our new television set works just as good/well as our old one.

ANSWER: Our new television set works just as <u>well</u> as our old one.

1. Rose always does good/well work.
2. I was bad/badly frightened by that story.
3. You drew those posters very good/well.
4. I felt very bad/badly when I learned you were ill.
5. It's a good/well thing you brought an umbrella.

Underline the correct adverb in each sentence.

EXAMPLE: I didn't get any/no apples at the store.

ANSWER: I didn't get <u>any</u> apples at the store.

6. She was not able to tell nobody/anybody about the surprise.
7. I never went nowhere/anywhere outside the United States.
8. He didn't do nothing/anything for the club.
9. She wasn't nowhere/anywhere near the finish line.
10. He can't do nothing/anything right.

Rewrite the following sentences so that there are no dangling or misplaced modifiers. (There may be more than one possible answer.)

EXAMPLE: Growing in the middle of the pond, she enjoyed looking at the water lilies.

ANSWER: She enjoyed looking at the water lilies growing in the middle of the pond.

11. While putting the turkey in the oven, the phone rang.
12. I borrowed a radio from my sister with an antenna.
13. At five years of age, my father taught me to play baseball.
14. Standing on her toes, we watched the ballerina.
15. I read about the thieves who were captured in this morning's paper.
16. On the bottom shelf of the refrigerator, I could not find the butter.

Diagramming a sentence shows the relationship of the words to the sentence as a whole. Every word has its own designated space in a diagram. When diagramming, capitalization is retained while punctuation is omitted.

SIMPLE SENTENCES

To diagram, start with a horizontal line called the baseline. The simple subject and simple predicate are placed on this line and are separated by a vertical line that cuts through the baseline.

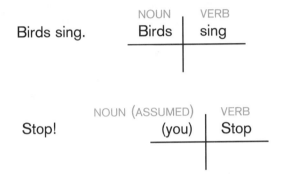

Birds sing.

Stop!

COMPOUND SUBJECTS AND COMPOUND VERBS

Each of the parts of the compound subject or verb is placed on a separate and parallel line. The lines are connected by a dotted line on which the conjunction or conjunctions joining them are placed.

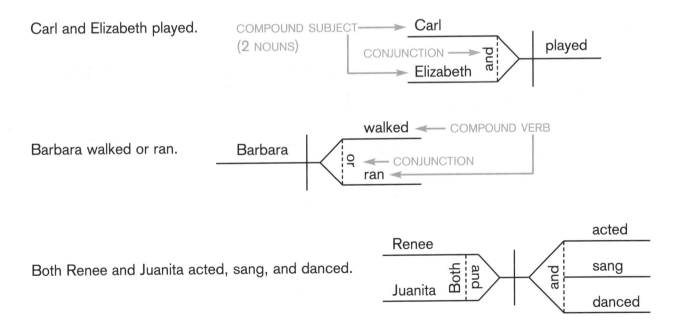

Carl and Elizabeth played.

Barbara walked or ran.

Both Renee and Juanita acted, sang, and danced.

ADJECTIVES AND ADVERBS

An adjective or adverb is placed on a diagonal line under the word that it modifies.

The very tall giraffe moved quite gracefully.

giraffe | moved

The — ADJECTIVE (ARTICLE)
very — ADVERB
tall — ADJECTIVE
quite — ADVERB
gracefully — ADVERB

Where are you going?

you | are going
Where — INTERROGATIVE ADVERB

Why did you come?

you | did come
Why — INTERROGATIVE ADVERB

INTERJECTIONS

Place the interjection on a horizontal line above the subject.

Oh my, it's a hot day!

Oh my ← INTERJECTION

it | is | day
a hot

NOTE: *When diagramming, treat a contraction as if it were the two words from which it was formed.*

DIRECT AND INDIRECT OBJECTS

A direct object is placed to the right of the verb and is separated from the verb by a vertical line.

Matthew threw the basketball.

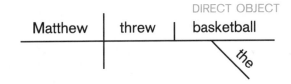

An indirect object is placed on a horizontal line parallel to the baseline and is linked to the verb by a diagonal line.

Matthew threw Charlie the basketball.

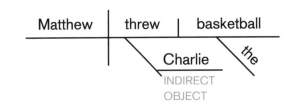

What can I do?

OBJECT AND SUBJECT COMPLEMENTS

An object complement is placed after the direct object on the baseline, with a diagonal line separating it from the direct object.

My mother considers my room messy.

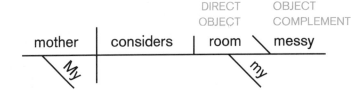

A subject complement is placed on the baseline to the right of the verb and is separated by a diagonal line.

Bruce is a pianist.

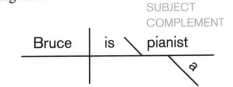

PREPOSITIONS AND PREPOSITIONAL PHRASES

The preposition is placed on a diagonal line under the word it modifies.

The object of the preposition is placed on a line connected to the preposition line and parallel to the baseline. Any word that modifies the object of the preposition is placed on a diagonal line under the word it modifies.

The treasure was found on the island under the palm tree.

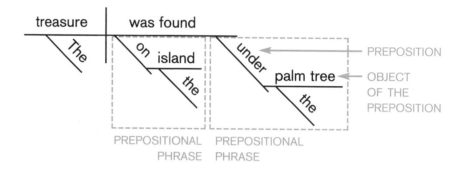

APPOSITIVES AND APPOSITIVE PHRASES

An appositive is placed beside the noun or pronoun it identifies. The appositive has parentheses placed around it.

My friend Paula is shy.

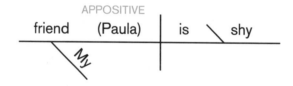

In an appositive phrase, place the words that modify the appositive on diagonal lines under the appositive.

Irene, a great beauty, lit up the room.

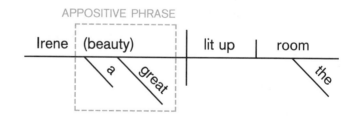

PARTICIPLES AND PARTICIPIAL PHRASES

A participle occupies both a diagonal line and a horizontal line under the word it modifies.

They left the sinking ship.

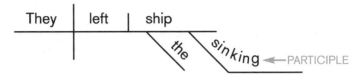

To diagram a participial phrase, place the participle as described above. If there is an object of the participle, place it to the right of the participle separated by a vertical line. Place modifiers as usual.

Looking for peace and quiet, I found a lovely garden.

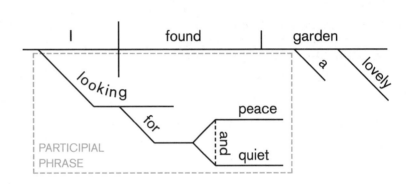

GERUNDS AND GERUND PHRASES

A gerund is placed on a stepped line on top of a stilt-like line in the noun space.

Cooking is Laura's passion.

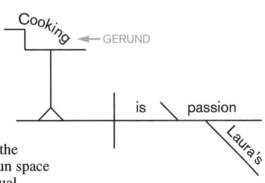

To diagram a gerund phrase, place the gerund on a stilt-like line in the noun space and diagram its complements as usual.

Walking to the store took fifteen minutes.

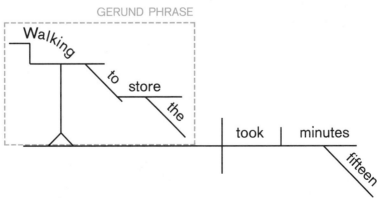

INFINITIVES AND INFINITIVE PHRASES

Diagram an infinitive, or an infinitive phrase that functions as an adverb or an adjective, as you would diagram a prepositional phrase.

The child felt the urge to jump.

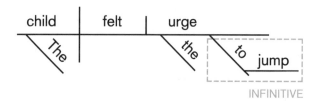

Diagram an infinitive, or an infinitive phrase that functions as a noun, as you would diagram a prepositional phrase, but place it on a stilt.

To prepare thoroughly is always a good idea.

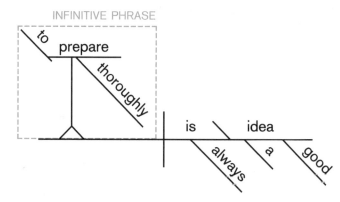

ABSOLUTE PHRASES

An absolute phrase is placed above the diagrammed sentence and is not connected to the main diagram. The subject of the phrase is on a horizontal line and the modifiers are diagrammed as usual.

With the stars so bright, it was a perfect night to study the constellations.

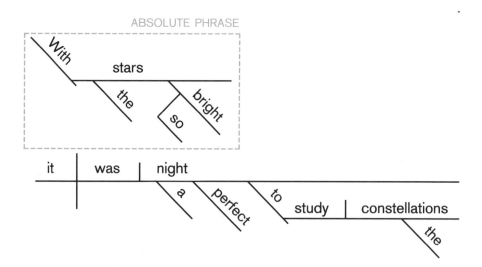

ADJECTIVE CLAUSES

An adjective clause is placed under the main diagram and is connected by a dotted line between the noun or pronoun being modified in the main clause and the introductory word of the clause.

A person who values his money will not squander it.

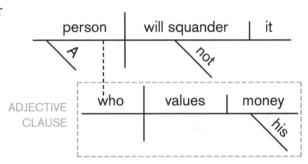

The actor who won the award could not remember his speech.

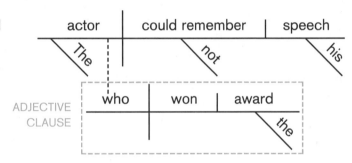

ADVERB CLAUSES

An adverb clause is placed under the main diagram and is connected by a diagonal dotted line between the word being modified in the main clause and the verb in the clause. The subordinating conjunction is placed on the dotted diagonal line.

The fire drill started when the alarm rang.

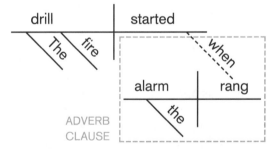

Diagram an elliptical adverb clause as you would an adverb clause with the understood words in parentheses.

I try to take time to smell the roses when in the garden.

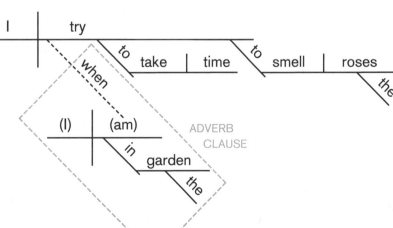

NOUN CLAUSES

Diagram the main clause as usual. Place the noun clause on a stilt-like line in the appropriate position. If the introductory word of the clause is a part of the clause, diagram it appropriately. If the introductory word of the clause is a connective word, place this it on a horizontal line above the verb in the noun clause and connect it to the verb in the noun clause with a dotted line.

The artist demonstrated how paint was mixed.

She gave a new book to whoever came early.

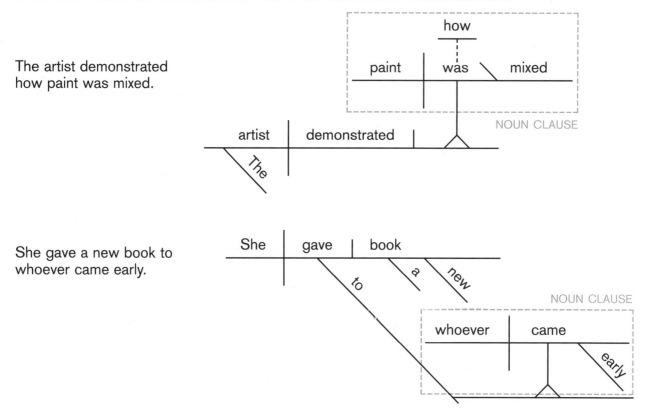

COMPOUND SENTENCES

Each clause in a compound sentence is diagrammed separately. If the clauses are connected by a conjunction, place the conjunction on a solid horizontal line between the clauses. This horizontal line is connected by dotted vertical lines to the verb of each clause. If a colon or semicolon connects the clauses, join the clauses with a dotted vertical line connecting the verb of each clause.

Dan sets the table and his sister washes the dishes.

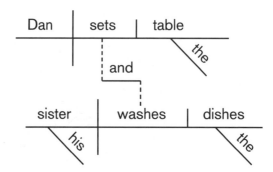

COMPOUND-COMPLEX SENTENCES

Diagram as you would a compound sentence.

Sally, who is a very busy woman, teaches three classes each day and conducts the orchestra.

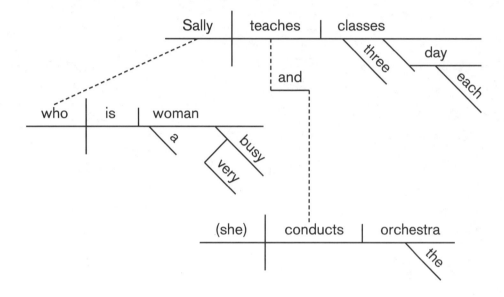

CAPITALIZATION

21

ALWAYS CAPITALIZE:

the pronoun I	You and I left the building together.	
proper nouns	New York Leslie Baustista	Lincoln Memorial Neptune
proper adjectives	American heritage Greek mythology	Italian food Irish music
days of the week	Sunday	Monday	Tuesday
months of the year	January	February	March
nationalities and people	Jamaicans	Russians	Puerto Ricans
languages	Polish	Chinese	English
religions	Christianity	Buddhism	Judaism
names of the deity	Lord Allah	God Vishnu	Our Father Zeus
holidays, religious days, and special events	Labor Day Easter	Fourth of July Kentucky Derby
streets and avenues	Fifth Avenue I live at 123 Main Street. The main street in our town is Elton Boulevard.	Peach Tree Lane
organizations	Bronx Zoo Elmdale Historical Society The Democratic Party is having a fund-raiser tonight. We live in a democratic society.	Peace Corps First National Bank
monuments and structures	Statue of Liberty Golden Gate Bridge That bridge reminds me of London Bridge. The Tomb of the Unknown Soldier is in Arlington Cemetery. The name of the soldier in the tomb is not known.	Eiffel Tower Empire State Building

continued on next page

ALWAYS CAPITALIZE: continued from previous page

historical documents	Emancipation Proclamation	Bill of Rights
	Magna Carta	the Constitution
	The Declaration of Independence was signed in Philadelphia.	
	I am declaring my independence from my parents.	
awards	Academy Award	Certificate of Excellence
	She won the Academic Achievement Award.	
	She won an award for academic achievement.	
titles before a proper name	Mrs. Josephine Berical	Chief Geronimo
	I have heard that President Washington was a tall man.	
	George Washington was the first U.S. president.	

The first word of a direct quotation should always be capitalized.

EXAMPLE: She told her students, "You have made me so proud."

The first word of each line of poetry usually begins with a capital letter.

EXAMPLE: Two roads diverged in a yellow wood,
And sorry I could not travel both
And be one traveler, long I stood
And looked down one as far as I could
To where it bent in the undergrowth;

excerpt from "The Road Not Taken"
by Robert Frost

Use a capital letter for the first word and for all words except articles, coordinating conjunctions, and prepositions of fewer than five letters in the title of a book, newspaper, magazine, song, poem, play, short story, movie, or television show.

EXAMPLES: A Tale of Two Cities
"Twinkle, Twinkle, Little Star"
Meet the Press

WHAT ABOUT ITALICS?

Italic is a printer's term for type that is slightly slanted.

Italicize or underline titles of longer works, such as: **books**, **magazines**, **newspapers**, **plays**, **movies**, **television series**, **operas or other named musical compositions**. Italics are also used for **foreign words or expressions**.

NOTE: The word Bible is always capitalized and never italicized.

PUNCTUATION

Every sentence should end with the correct punctuation mark. Punctuation marks include the period, the question mark, and the exclamation point.

PERIOD

A period (.) is used to end a **declarative** or **imperative** sentence.

> EXAMPLES: He ran to catch the ball.
> Tell me what to do.

A period is used after an **initial** in a proper noun.

> EXAMPLES: John F. Kennedy
> Susan B. Anthony
> P. T. Barnum

A period is used at the end of an **abbreviation**.

QUESTION MARK

A question mark (?) is used at the end of an **interrogative** sentence.

> EXAMPLE: How may I help you?

A question mark is used to indicate a direct question quoted within a declarative sentence.

> EXAMPLE: "How are you today?" she asked her mother.

EXCLAMATION POINT

An exclamation point (!) is used to end an **exclamatory** sentence. An exclamation point is used to show strong feeling or to indicate a forceful **command** or **imperative**.

> EXAMPLES: That play was wonderful!
> Get out of the street!

An exclamation point is used after an **interjection**. An interjection is an unrelated word or phrase that expresses an emotion or exclamation.

> EXAMPLES: Hooray! Our team won the race.
> Wow! That ride was fun.

SOME COMMON ABBREVIATIONS			
January	Jan.	February	Feb.
March	Mar.	April	Apr.
August	Aug.	September	Sept.
October	Oct.	November	Nov.
December	Dec.	Sunday	Sun.
Monday	Mon.	Tuesday	Tues.
Wednesday	Wed.	Thursday	Thurs.
Friday	Fri.	Saturday	Sat.
Avenue	Ave.	Drive	Dr.
Street	St.	Place	Pl.
Highway	Hwy.	Boulevard	Blvd.
Road	Rd.	Mister	Mr.
Senior	Sr.	Junior	Jr.
Reverend	Rev.	Father	Fr.
Doctor	Dr.	Director	Dir.
foot	ft.	gallon	gal.

COMMA

A comma (,) is used:

- between the main clauses in a compound sentence.
  EXAMPLE: Today is Jack's birthday, and his family is taking him to the circus.

- before the conjunction **and**, **but**, **or**, **nor**, or **for** when it joins two main clauses.
  EXAMPLE: She liked to watch television, but she also enjoyed reading.

- to separate three or more groups of words, phrases, or clauses in a series.
  EXAMPLE: The salad was made with tomatoes, onions, celery, and peppers.

- to separate adjectives that modify the same noun to an equal degree.
  EXAMPLE: The spring plants grew with small, tender leaf buds.

- before a direct quotation.
  EXAMPLE: Susan asked, "What time is it?"

- to separate a direct quotation from other words in the sentence.
  EXAMPLE: "He knew my father," said Mark, "but he has never met my uncle."

- to separate words or names used in direct address.
  EXAMPLE: Matthew, did you get your report card yet?

- to set off participles, infinitives, and their phrases if they are not essential to the meaning of the sentence.
  EXAMPLE: Billy, who is always prompt, was delayed by snow today.

- to set off interjections, parenthetical expressions, and conjunctive adverbs.
  EXAMPLE: Oh my, I had no idea you were coming.

Do not use a comma between a subject and its verb or a verb and its object.

ALSO USE A COMMA:

• after a salutation in a friendly letter and after the close of a letter.	Dear Mommy, Dear Bobby, Sincerely,
• to set off a title when it follows a person's name	Stanley Yankelowitz, M.D. Steven Schwabe, D.D.S.
• between the name of a city and a state.	Albany, New York Ames, Iowa
• in a date, to set off the year, when both the month and date are used.	March 30, 1986 March 1986 March 30
• to set off parts of a reference.	Encyclopedia, book 4, pages 45-78 Romeo and Juliet, Act 1, Scene 2

SEMICOLON

The semicolon (;) is used:

- to separate main clauses that are **not** joined by the conjunctions **and**, **but**, **or**, **nor**, **for** or **yet**.
  EXAMPLE: His car will not start; he needs to call his mechanic.

- to separate main clauses joined by a **conjunctive adverb** (such as however, therefore, nevertheless, moreover, furthermore, subsequently, and consequently) or by an expression such as **for example** or **that is**.
  EXAMPLE: My exams begin on Tuesday; therefore, I must study this weekend.

- to separate items in a series when these items already contain commas.
  EXAMPLE: We visited Washington, D.C.; Atlanta, Georgia; and Orlando, Florida.

COLON

The colon (:) is used:

- to introduce a list, especially after a statement that uses the words: **as follows**, **the following**, **these**, **namely**, or **for example**.
  EXAMPLE: Science classes taught in my school are the following: biology, chemistry, physics, and earth science.

- to introduce material that illustrates, explains, or restates the preceding material.
  EXAMPLE: All of his energy was focussed on one objective: getting home.

- to introduce a long or formal quotation, often preceded by words as **this**, **these**, **the following**, or **as follows**.
  EXAMPLE: In 1776 the British hanged Nathan Hale as a spy. His last words were the following: "I only regret that I have but one life to give for my country."

- in a business letter salutation.
  EXAMPLE: Dear Mr. Liu:

- in biblical references, between chapter and verse.
  EXAMPLE: John 3:16

- between the hour and the minute of the precise time.
  EXAMPLE: 11:59 P.M.

QUOTATION MARKS

Quotation marks (" ") are used to enclose a **direct quotation** or the exact words of a speaker. Place the quotation marks around the quoted material only, not around the introductory remarks.

EXAMPLE: I asked her, "Are you going to sign up for any sports classes?"

If the quotation is interrupted by explanatory words such as **he said** or **she said**, use two sets of quotation marks. You must have the correct punctuation (such as a comma or a period) before and after the explanatory or interrupting words.

EXAMPLE: "Who," he asked, "is reponsible for this project?"

Do not use quotation marks in an indirect quotation.

EXAMPLE: They announced that they were getting married.

Quotation marks are also used:

- to refer to the titles of short works, such as short stories, short poems, songs, or newspaper articles.

  EXAMPLES: "The Tiger" (poem)
  "Ode to Joy" (song)

- to enclose unusual expressions or slang.

  EXAMPLE: In England they call an elevator a "lift."

- to enclose definitions.

  EXAMPLE: Grammar is, "the study of the classes of words, their inflections and their functions and relations in a sentence."

SINGLE QUOTATION MARKS

Use single quotation marks (' ') for a quotation within a quotation.

EXAMPLE: "Can we sing 'Yellow Submarine' in music class?" asked the student.

WATCH OUT!

Single quotation marks look just like **apostrophes**. You use the same key to type them, but they are used very differently.

QUOTATION MARKS AND OTHER PUNCTUATION

Always place a comma or a period inside closing quotation marks.

EXAMPLE: Shakespeare's Hamlet will always be remembered for saying, "To be or not to be, that is the question."

Always place a semicolon or a colon outside closing quotation marks.

EXAMPLE: I never understood Lincoln's opening remarks in the Gettysburg Address, "Four score and seven years ago"; then I learned that the word score means twenty.

When a question mark or exclamation point is part of a quotation, place it inside closing quotation marks.

EXAMPLE: I like the advertisement that asks, "Where's the beef?"

When a question mark or exclamation point is part of the entire sentence, place it outside closing quotation marks.

EXAMPLE: Why does Jimmy always say, "I want to go to the park"?

APOSTROPHE

An apostrophe (') is used to form possessive nouns and contractions.

THE APOSTROPHE IS USED:

in the place of the first two numerals of a year	the summer of '99 class of '08
to show ownership:	
• of a singular noun not ending in s or an s sound by adding 's.	anyone's bicycle Maria's restaurant
• of a singular noun of one syllable ending in s or an s sound by adding 's.	boss's office fox's den
• of a singular noun ending in s or an s sound by adding either 's or '. If the next word begins with a s add '.	Beatrice' or Beatrice's bike octopus' or octopus's tentacles hostess' or hostess's charm hostess' seat
• of a singular noun in a plural form by adding '.	mathematics' rules measles' shot
• with proper names ending is s by using '.	Socrates' ideas Dickens' stories
• of a plural noun not ending in s by adding 's.	firemen's coats children's museum
• of a plural noun ending in s by adding '.	families' photograph teams' basketball
• of a compound noun at the end of the compound word.	mother-in-law's house Secretary General's report

CONTRACTIONS

A contraction is a shortened form of two words. The apostrophe (') takes the place of one or more letters.

EXAMPLES:
Do not go there.   Don't go there.
It is a nice day.   It's a nice day.
You must not eat those.   You mustn't eat those.

COMMON CONTRACTIONS

CONTRACTION	FORMED FROM	CONTRACTION	FORMED FROM
I'm	I am	we're	we are
I've	I have	we've	we have
I'd	I had/I would	we'd	we had/we would
I'll	I will	we'll	we will
he's	he is/he has	you're	you are
she's	she is/she has	you've	you have
it's	it is/it has	you'd	you had/you would
he'd	he had/he would	you'll	you will
she'd	she had/she would	they're	they are
he'll	he will	they've	they have
she'll	she will	they'd	they had/they would

NOTE: **'s** can stand for **is** or **has**, and **'d** can stand for **had** or **would**.

WATCH OUT!

Its is the possessive form of it.
It's is a contraction of it is or it has.

Your is the possessive form of you.
You're is a contraction of you are.

HYPHEN

THE HYPHEN (-) IS USED:

• to join a prefix to a proper noun or proper adjective and after the prefixes **all-**, **ex-** (meaning former), **anti-** (when it joins a word beginning with i), **self-** (joined to any noun or adjective), **vice-** (except in vice president).	all-American ex-president anti-inflammatory self-confident vice-chancellor
• in a compound adjective that precedes a noun. Use a hyphen in compound adjectives beginning with **well**, **ill**, and **little** except when they are modifying an adverb.	red-colored dress well-known commentator little-known restaurant ill-fated expedition
• in cardinal or ordinary numbers that are spelled out up to ninety-nine or ninety-ninth.	twenty-one thirty-fifth
• in fractions expressed in words.	one-half teaspoon one-half cup
• to separate two numerals in a span.	1886-1889 pages 4-11

The hyphen is also used to divide words between syllables at the end of the written or printed line.

WORD	CAN BE DIVIDED		
benefit	ben-efit	or	bene-fit
fatherly	fa-therly	or	father-ly
informal	in-formal	or	infor-mal
merchandise	mer-chandise	or	merchan-dise
syllables	syl-lables	or	sylla-bles
achievement	achieve-ment		
hyphen	hy-phen		
lighthouse	light-house		
sequence	se-quence		

WHEN IN DOUBT...

Consult a dictionary to verify:
- whether a word requires a hyphen
  or
- where the syllable breaks occur.

PARENTHESES

Parentheses ( ) are used to set off supplemental material that is not important enough to be considered part of the main sentence.

EXAMPLES: IBM (International Business Machines) is a large company.
George Washington (1732-1799) was the first president of the United States.

A complete sentence within parentheses does not need capitalization or end punctuation if it is part of a larger sentence.

EXAMPLE: Tom (he has a great imagination) has written three books.

If a sentence in parentheses stands by itself, use both capital letter and end punctuation.

EXAMPLE: Lewis and Clark were commissioned by President Thomas Jefferson to explore the American West. (For more information, consult your local library.)

DASH

The dash (—) is used mostly in informal personal letters. The dash is the size of two hyphens.

A dash is used to:

- indicate an abrupt break or change in thought within a sentence.
  EXAMPLE: I was reading a book—suddenly all the alarms went off.

- emphasize an appositive or to set off a series of them.
  EXAMPLE: I will be taking a class with the piano teacher—Mr. Govin.

- emphasize a parenthetical clause or extra information.
  EXAMPLE: Susan and John went to a movie—Casablanca—on Friday.

- show hesitation.
  EXAMPLE: But—I'm sure I sent it.

Do not use a comma, semicolon, colon, or period before or after a dash.

ELLIPSIS POINTS

Ellipsis points (…) are used to indicate an omission of material from a quotation. When used at the end of a sentence use the three points plus a period.

EXAMPLES: Neil Armstrong said, when he landed on the moon, "One small step for man…."
Patrick Henry said, "…give me liberty or give me death!"

PARAGRAPHS

Longer pieces of writing are divided up into smaller sections called paragraphs.

A paragraph is a group of sentences presented in a logical order for ease of reading and comprehension. Each paragraph should focus on a single topic. Each paragraph contains a topic sentence that states the main idea of the paragraph and supporting sentences that provide additional detail. A paragraph may be as short as a single sentence. Start a new paragraph each time you begin a new topic. This alerts the reader that a new idea is being introduced.

There are two styles generally used to indicate the beginning of a new paragraph. Either indent the first line of each new paragraph or add a line between paragraphs and do not indent.

EXAMPLE:

David, Warner, and Jeanie boarded the A train to Coney Island. They brought their bags, stuffed with swimming suits, Frisbees, and suntan lotion, with them. On the train they talked excitedly about what they would be doing when they got to their destination. They saw lots of other passengers who were also going to Coney Island.

After leaving the subway station, they headed straight for the beach. They quickly changed into their swimming suits, put on their suntan lotion, and jumped into the crashing waves. They stayed at the beach until sunset, alternately swimming and throwing the Frisbee back and forth among themselves.

After changing out of their swimsuits and into their regular clothes, they went to the amusement park. David suggested that they go to the Wonder Wheel first. They got lost in the hall of mirrors and rode the Cyclone roller coaster twice. Jeanie won a huge stuffed animal at a game booth. Later, Warner bought cotton candy for everyone.

At midnight, they went home exhausted.

NOTE: *In each of the above four paragraphs a single topic is addressed. Each paragraph describes a separate part of the day. The topic sentence of each paragraph is the first sentence of the paragraph. The supporting sentences complete the story begun in the topic sentence.*

PRACTICE

Divide the following text into shorter paragraphs. Indicate where you believe a new paragraph should begin by circling the appropriate number sign. Remember, each new paragraph should address a new topic.

The Hernandez children had a wonderful day. (1) In the morning, they went to the local park. (2) While they were there, they played in the playground.(3) Fernando played basketball with his dad. (4) Jessica slid down the slide numerous times. (5) Asiria's mom pushed her on the swings. (6) When they were hungry, they ate the picnic lunch that their mother had made for them. (7) After lunch, they played tag, catch, and hide-and-seek. (8) Later that day, they went to the movie theater to see a movie. (9) They had to decide which movie to see. (10) Fernando wanted to see a movie about dinosaurs. (11) Jessica and Asiria wanted to see an animated movie. (12) They finally agreed to see a comedy about a family that had too many pets. (13) All three children enjoyed the movie very much. (14) The Hernandez family went to their favorite restaurant for dinner that evening. (15) The father ordered a steak and a baked potato. (16) The mother ordered pork chops and a salad. (17) Fernando and Jessica ordered cheeseburgers with french fries. (18) Asiria ordered a personal-sized pepperoni pizza. (19) For dessert they all had hot apple pie with a scoop of ice cream on top. (20) The delicious meal made a wonderful day even better.

BUSINESS LETTERS

Business letters are usually typed on 8 1/2" X 11" paper or stationery.

In writing an effective business letter it is important to communicate your message in a concise and straightforward manner. Try to keep your sentences short and clear.

The opening paragraph should state the purpose of the letter. In the middle paragraph, or paragraphs, go into more detail. In the closing paragraph, restate the purpose of the letter and tell how to communicate with you.

heading:
your address
date of letter

Widget World
123 Riverview Drive
Anywhere, NY 12345
March 17, 2000

inside address:
name
title
company
address

Tom Smith
Vice President
Widgets Corporation
789 Main St
Anywhere, NY 12345

salutation

Dear Mr. Smith:

body of the letter

Our company is interested in ordering a large number of widgets. We are especially interested in your new line of whirling widgets for industrial use.

Please send us your complete catalogue and price list. We also would appreciate receiving information about your other products.

We look forward to hearing from you. If you have any questions regarding this request, please call me at (123) 456-7890.

closing

Sincerely,

your signature

Joseph Jones

your typed name

Joseph Jones

PERSONAL LETTERS

Personal letters are frequently handwritten.

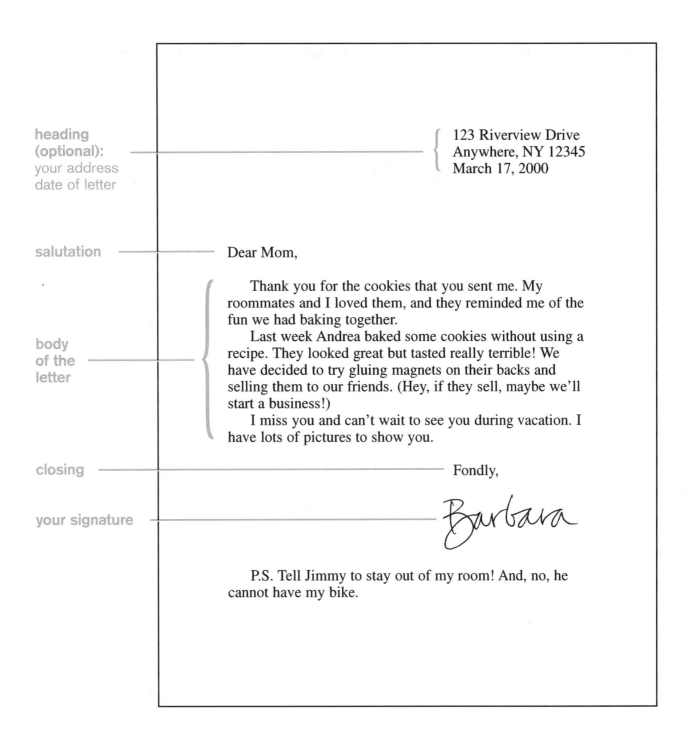

heading
(optional):
your address
date of letter

123 Riverview Drive
Anywhere, NY 12345
March 17, 2000

salutation

Dear Mom,

body
of the
letter

    Thank you for the cookies that you sent me. My roommates and I loved them, and they reminded me of the fun we had baking together.
    Last week Andrea baked some cookies without using a recipe. They looked great but tasted really terrible! We have decided to try gluing magnets on their backs and selling them to our friends. (Hey, if they sell, maybe we'll start a business!)
    I miss you and can't wait to see you during vacation. I have lots of pictures to show you.

closing

Fondly,

your signature

Barbara

    P.S. Tell Jimmy to stay out of my room! And, no, he cannot have my bike.

25 COMMON MISTAKES

ACCEPT / EXCEPT

Accept means to give an affirmative answer or to receive. **Except** means to exclude or with the exclusion of.

EXAMPLES: They accepted the award.

The entire family, except Donna, went to the wedding.

ADVICE / ADVISE

Advice is a noun that means an opinion, information. **Advise** is a verb that means to counsel, recommend, or suggest.

EXAMPLES: On the advice of my teacher, I study every day.

My Dad advised me to study.

AFFECT / EFFECT

Affect is a verb that means to have an influence on, or cause a change in. As a noun, **effect** means an end result or consequence. As a verb, it means to produce or bring about.

EXAMPLES: The move to San Diego affected the entire family.

The rain had a direct effect on the picnic. (noun)

The sudden rainfall effected a change in the river. (verb)

AIN'T

Ain't is slang. Don't use it. It is slang for **are not**, **is not**, or **am not**.

EXAMPLES: We are not going to use slang words.

It is not my wish to sound uneducated.

I am not going to use slang words.

ALL TOGETHER / ALTOGETHER

All together means everything or everyone at once. As an adverb, **altogether** means completely or thoroughly.

EXAMPLES: The class went all together on the field trip.

Altogether there were nineteen children on the bus.

ALLUSION / ILLUSION

Allusion means an indirect reference or casual mention. **Illusion** means an unreal image or a false idea.

EXAMPLES: Elizabeth, in her speech, made an allusion to Mark Twain.

The speaker gave the illusion of confidence, until the audience questioned him.

ALOT / A LOT / ALLOT

There is no such word as **alot**. **A lot** is a noun meaning a great quantity. **Allot** is a verb meaning to assign as a share or portion.

EXAMPLES: There is a lot of water in the pool.

The speakers are allotted ten minutes each.

ALREADY / ALL READY

Already is an adverb meaning by this time or previously. **All ready** is a phrase meaning completely prepared.

EXAMPLES: We had already baked a pie for the picnic.
Now that we have finished packing, we are all ready to leave.

ALRIGHT / ALL RIGHT

There is no such word as **alright**. **All right** means every thing is correct.

EXAMPLE: Every thing will be all right.

ALTAR / ALTER

Altar is a noun meaning a table of worship. **Alter** is a verb meaning to change.

EXAMPLES: This church has a lovely altar.
The tailor will alter the suit.

AMONG / BETWEEN

Among refers to more than two individuals or items. **Between** refers to only two individuals or items.

EXAMPLES: The reward was shared among Tom, Dick, and Harry.
I had to choose between ice cream and cake.

AMOUNT / NUMBER

Amount refers to things in bulk. **Number** refers to things that can be counted.

EXAMPLES: The beach has a large amount of white sand.
A small number of my classmates went on the field trip.

ANYONE / ANY ONE

Anyone refers to any person at all. **Any one** refers to a particular person.

EXAMPLES: Anyone can try out for the team.
Any one of us could win the race.

ASCENT /ASSENT

Ascent is a noun meaning the act of rising. **Assent** can be used as a verb or as a noun meaning agreement.

EXAMPLES: The ascent of Mt. Everest is difficult and dangerous.
The council assented to the proposal. (verb)
The council gave its assent to the proposal. (noun)

BAD / BADLY

Bad is an adjective. **Badly** is an adverb.
EXAMPLES: Tom is a bad sailor.
Tom sails badly.

BETWEEN YOU AND I / BETWEEN YOU AND ME

Between you and I is incorrect. **Between you and me** is correct because me is the object of the preposition.
EXAMPLE: Keep this secret between you and me.

BRING / TAKE

Bring shows movement toward the speaker. **Take** indicates movement away from the speaker.
EXAMPLES: Bring the map with you when you come to visit me.
Take the map with you when you go on your trip.

CAN / MAY

Can means the ability to do something. **May** is used to ask permission.
EXAMPLES: I can play tennis.
Mom, may I go to the park?

CAPITAL / CAPITOL

Capital can be used as a noun refering to the city that is the seat of government or to money, or as an adjective meaning most serious. Capital also means upper case. **Capitol** is used to refer to a government building.
EXAMPLES: Denver is the capital of Colorado. (noun)
A sentence always begins with a capital letter. (adjective)
We visited the capitol building in Atlanta.

CHOSE / CHOOSE

Chose is the past tense of the verb **choose**.
EXAMPLES: Paula chose to take a computer class last year.
Carla must choose between the two candidates.

COMPLEMENT / COMPLIMENT

Complement is a noun or a verb meaning to complete or make perfect. **Compliment** is a noun or a verb meaning to praise or admire.
EXAMPLES: The ice cream was a perfect complement to the apple pie. (noun)
The color of your shirt complements your eyes. (verb)
Please take this gift with my compliments. (noun)
I must compliment you on the great party you gave. (verb)

COULD OF / COULD HAVE

There is no such phrase as **could of**, use **could have** or the contraction **could've**.

EXAMPLE: We could have (could've) played all day.

COUNCIL / COUNSEL

Council is a noun meaning an assembly of people. **Counsel** can be a verb meaning to give advice or a noun, meaning guarded thoughts.

EXAMPLES: The council will vote tomorrow.
He counseled his children to study hard. (verb)
It is wise to keep one's own counsel. (noun)

E.G. / I.E.

The notation **e.g.** means for example. It is the abbreviation of the Latin *exempli gratia*. The notation **i.e.** means that is (to say). It is the abbreviation of the Latin *id est*. E.g. and i.e. should be proceeded and followed by commas.

EXAMPLES: My sister likes flowers that smell fragrant, e.g., roses, and lilacs.
We are studying the life of our first president, i.e., George Washington.

ELICIT / ILLICIT

Elicit means to bring out or to draw forth. **Illicit** refers to something illegal.

EXAMPLES: Sherlock Holmes was able to elicit information from a variety of sources.
The smugglers were involved in illicit activities.

EMIGRATE / IMMIGRATE

Emigrate means to leave one country or region to live in another. **Immigrate** means to enter and live in a country or region to which one is not a native.

EXAMPLES: My grandfather emigrated from Ireland.
My grandfather immigrated to the United States.

EMINENT / IMMINENT / IMMANENT

Eminent means distinguished. **Imminent** means about to occur or impending. **Immanent** means existing or remaining within, inherent.

EXAMPLES: The speaker at our assembly is an eminent educator.
As the hurricane approached, we were in imminent danger.
The family's immanent faith was evident in their charitable works.

ET AL. / ETC.

The notation **et al.** means and others. It is the abbreviation of the Latin *et alia*. The notation **etc.** means and other things. It is the abbreviation of the word etcetera.

EXAMPLES: The article was written by Smith, Riley, Daniels, et al.
She came with a large bag filled with cookies, ice cream, cake, etc.

ENVELOP / ENVELOPE

Envelop is a verb that means to enfold, enclose, or cover. **Envelope** is a noun that refers to something enclosing or surrounding by means of a cover, coat, or wrapping.

EXAMPLES: The fog seemed to envelop the entire area.
The envelope was addressed to occupant.

FARTHER / FURTHER

Farther means at or to a greater distance. **Further** means more or increased in time or degree.

EXAMPLES: Because it was such a nice day, we walked farther than we had planned.
The science project calls for further experimentation.

FAZE / PHASE

Faze is a verb meaning to disrupt the composure of, or to disturb. **Phase** is a noun meaning a distinct stage of development or a temporary pattern of behavior.

EXAMPLES: I am so used to the noise that it does not faze me at all.
Every mother dreads the phase of childhood known as the "terrible twos."

FEWER / LESS

Fewer means consisting of a small number that is capable of being counted. **Less** means to a smaller extent, degree, or frequency.

EXAMPLES: There are fewer children in my class than in my sister's class.
Now that I am older, it takes me less time to walk to school.

FLAUNT / FLOUT

Flaunt means to exhibit ostentatiously or to show off. **Flout** means to scorn, mock, or defy.

EXAMPLES: He flaunted his wealth by driving his expensive new car up and down the street.
They flouted the rules by climbing the fence.

GOOD / WELL

Good is an adjective. **Well** is an adverb.

EXAMPLES: It was a good idea to come here.
The children are behaving well.

INFER / IMPLY

Infer means to draw a conclusion from facts or to deduce. **Imply** means to indicate by allusion or to express indirectly.

> EXAMPLES: I infer from your cheering that you are a fan of the home team.
> His smile implied that he was happy with the gift.

IRREGARDLESS / REGARDLESS

There is no such word as **irregardless** use regardless. **Regardless** means heedless, or in spite of everything.

> EXAMPLE: Regardless of the weather, he walks ten miles every day.

ITS / IT'S

Its is a possessive pronoun showing ownership. **It's** is a contraction of the words it is.

> EXAMPLES: Put the book in its place.
> It's a fine day.

LEARN / TEACH

Learn means to acquire knowledge or information. **Teach** means to give knowledge or information.

> EXAMPLES: I want to learn more about American history.
> Mrs. Barker is going to teach a history class.

LIE / LAY

The verb **lie** means to rest or recline and never takes a direct object. The verb **lay** means to place and always takes a direct object.

> EXAMPLES: The doctor told the patient to lie down. (present tense of lie)
> She lay down and took a nap. (past tense of lie)
> Please lay your pencil on the table. (present tense of lay)
> The carpenter laid down his hammer. (past tense of lay)

LOOSE / LOSE

As an adjective, **loose** means less tight. **Lose** is a verb meaning to misplace or to be unable to maintain something.

> EXAMPLES: This screw is loose.
> Be careful not to lose your balance on the slippery sidewalk.

MAY BE / MAYBE

May be is a verb phrase. **Maybe** is an adverb meaning perhaps.

> EXAMPLES: It may be a good time to go home.
> Maybe we should go home.

MYSELF

Myself is a reflexive or intensive pronoun. Never use myself to replace I or me.

EXAMPLES: I drove myself to school.
I ran in the marathon myself.

PASSED / PAST

Passed is the past tense of the verb pass meaning to go by. **Past** is a noun, an adjective, or a preposition referring to time gone by.

EXAMPLES: On our way home we passed the library.
The past four years have been happy ones. (adjective)
His past is a secret. (noun)
We drove past the library. (preposition)

PRINCIPAL / PRINCIPLE

Principal can be an adjective or a noun. As an adjective, it means chief or chief official. As a noun, it means a person who holds rank, a main participant, or a sum of money. **Principle** is a noun meaning fundamental truth.

EXAMPLES: We studied the principal parts of verbs in class today. (adjective)
Our school principal inspired us to succeed. (noun)
One of the main principles of democracy is that all men are created equal.

RECUR / REOCCUR

There is no such word as **reoccur**. **Recur** means to happen, come up, or show up repeatedly.

EXAMPLE: The spring floods recur every year.

REGIME / REGIMEN

Regime refers to a form of rule or government. **Regimen** refers to any systematic plan.

EXAMPLES: The revolutionaries fought against the totalitarian regime.
My doctor advised me to begin a daily regimen of exercise.

RESPECTFULLY / RESPECTIVELY

Respectfully means in a manner showing esteem or honor. **Respectively** means in the order given.

EXAMPLES: The class respectfully listened to the teacher.
John and Michael played pitcher and catcher respectively.

STATIONARY / STATIONERY

Stationary means in a fixed position. **Stationery** refers to writing paper and envelopes.

EXAMPLES: The gym has a stationary bike.
I use fancy stationery to write to my pen pal.

THAN / THEN

Than is a conjunction used in comparative statements. **Then** can be an adverb or adverbial conjunction that relates to time.

EXAMPLES: I like chocolate ice cream better than vanilla.
First, you have to clean your room, then you can go to the movie.

THEIR / THERE / THEY'RE

Their is a pronoun that shows ownership. **There** indicates location. **They're** is a contraction of they are.

EXAMPLES: That is their home.
Plant the flowers there.
They're going to the mall.

TO / TOO / TWO

To is a preposition that shows direction. **Too** is an adverb that means also or an excessive degree. **Two** is a number.

EXAMPLES: We are going to a party.
There is no such thing as too much chocolate.
I have two dolls.

WEATHER / WHETHER

Weather refers to the atmosphere. **Whether** means if.

EXAMPLES: The weather in Arizona is usually hot and dry.
I plan to go whether it rains or not.

WHO / WHOM

Who is always the subject in the sentence. **Whom** is always the object in the sentence.

EXAMPLES: Who was here?
With whom is she dancing?

WHO'S / WHOSE

Who's is the contraction of who is. **Whose** is the possessive form of who.

EXAMPLES: Who's coming to the party.
Whose book is that?

YOUR / YOU'RE

Your is a possessive pronoun showing ownership. **You're** is a contraction of the words you are.

EXAMPLES: I just love your haircut.
You're going to be late.

COMMONLY MISPRONOUNCED WORDS

WORD	INCORRECT PRONUNCIATION	CORRECT PRONUNCIATION
ask	ax	ask
err	air	ur
etcetera	ek cet er a	et cet er a
February	Feb yu ary	Feb roo er e
integral	in tre gal	in te gral or in teg ral
length	lenth	length
library	li bary	li brary
mine	mines	mine
minuscule	min is cule	min us cule
oil	earl	oy ul
postpone	post fone	post pone
realtor	reel ah tor	reel tor
nuclear	nuc u lar	nu klee ar
recognize	rec o nize	rec og nize
says	says	sez
similar	sim u lar	sim i lar

COMMONLY MISPRONOUNCED EXPRESSIONS

EXPRESSION	INCORRECT PRONUNCIATION	EXPRESSION	INCORRECT PRONUNCIATION
going to	gonna	must have	musta
got to	gotta	should have	shoulda
has to	hasta	would have	woulda
have to	hafta	bet you	betcha
ought to	oughta	did you	didja
want to	wanna	get you	getcha
want to be	wannabe	got you	gotcha
kind of	kinda	don't you	doncha
kinds of	kindsa	what did you	whadja
lot of	lotta	give me	gimme
lots of	lotsa	let me	lemme
could have	coulda	I don't know	I dunno
might have	mighta		

ANSWERS TO PRACTICE QUESTIONS

CHAPTER 2, NOUNS, p. 6

1. The car <u>lights</u> are turned off. *common noun*
2. The new car belongs to <u>Doctor Riley</u>. *proper noun*
3. The lesson <u>Jeanne</u> studied was very interesting. *proper noun*
4. Is this <u>restaurant</u> closed? *common noun*
5. The <u>teacher</u> spoke with me. *common noun*

6. Some <u>people's</u> voices can always be heard.
7. That store sells <u>women's</u> shoes
8. Where are his <u>grandchildren's</u> toys?
9. <u>Gus'</u> car is being repaired.
10. The <u>birds'</u> nests are empty

	SINGULAR	PLURAL
11.	parade	parades
12.	fox	foxes
13.	room	rooms
14.	bush	bushes
15.	beach	beaches
16.	goose	geese
17.	housefly	horseflies
18.	man	men
19.	party	parties
20.	tooth	teeth

CHAPTER 3, PRONOUNS, pp. 10-11

1. <u>She</u> grows tomatoes every year.
2. <u>It</u> flew out of the nest.
3. <u>They</u> like to listen to music.
4. Will you bring a present for <u>him</u>?
5. Who bought <u>his</u> baseball ticket?

6. <u>You</u> must learn to drive carefully. *second person*
7. The <u>coach</u> taught them the merit of teamwork. *third person*
8. <u>I</u> am going to sing in the concert. *first person*
9. Will <u>you</u> teach me how to ski? *second person*
10. <u>Susan</u> has given us a lot of help. *third person*

11. <u>Mine</u> is the last one.
12. <u>My</u> cat is gray.
13. Are those tickets <u>theirs</u>?
14. <u>Its</u> sound is pleasant.
15. <u>Their</u> car is in the parking lot.

16. This is the road <u>that</u> goes to Anna's house.
17. My dog is three years old, <u>which</u> is like 21 in dog years.
18. This is my tennis coach Mary, <u>who</u> is also my best friend.
19. The flag will be carried by a student, <u>who</u> will become the class leader.
20. My juice is in a glass <u>that</u> is on the table.

21. <u>Whom</u> are you seeing today?
22. <u>Whom</u> did you invite to the party?
23. <u>Whose</u> work is complete?
24. Did you find out <u>who</u> gave you the tickets for the game?
25. <u>Whom</u> was he trying to call?
26. <u>Which</u> of the colors matches your eyes?
27. <u>Who</u> scored the winning run?
28. <u>What</u> is your name?
29. <u>Who</u> invented the radio?
30. <u>Whom</u> did you ask?
31. <u>Whose</u> idea was that?

32. <u>This</u> is a favorite photo. *demonstrative*
33. Tony will go the store <u>himself</u>. *reflexive*
34. <u>Her</u> dog does tricks. *possessive*
35. Does <u>anyone</u> want milk? *indefinite*
36. Laura <u>herself</u> fixed the leak. *intensive*
37. Bernie has two of <u>those</u> at home. *demonstrative*
38. <u>They</u> are always together. *personal*
39. <u>Something</u> is wrong with the telephone. *indefinite*
40. <u>Their</u> car is green. *possessive*
41. <u>Which</u> one did Wendy buy? *interrogative*
42. <u>We</u> are lab partners. *personal*
43. <u>That</u> movie was scary. *demonstrative*

CHAPTER 4, VERBS, pp. 14-15

1. All of us <u>enjoy</u> your stories.
2. You <u>read</u> many books this summer!
3. We <u>ride</u> the same bus to school every day.
4. I <u>think</u> about you often.
5. Their family <u>swims</u> at the beach in August.
6. The patient <u>feels</u> much better today.
7. We <u>have been</u> out for most of the day.
8. Dim lights <u>appeared</u> through the fog.
9. I <u>was</u> at the game last night.
10. The juniors and seniors <u>are</u> in the auditorium.

11. Kelly <u>is</u> studying for her next exam.
12. Carrie <u>has</u> driven the blue car for two years.
13. Chris <u>can</u> visit his parents every weekend.
14. Your car <u>was</u> towed away.
15. I <u>am</u> trying this new recipe.

16. I <u>must send</u> those packages soon.
17. The manager <u>will close</u> the store early today.
18. She <u>has been digging</u> in her garden all afternoon.
19. He <u>has heard</u> that story before.
20. Anthony <u>has closed</u> the door.

21. The lost child <u>sobbed</u> in the corner of the store. *intransitive*
22. Mrs. Griffin <u>pushed</u> the baby carriage down the street. *transitive*
23. They <u>ran</u> for hours. *intransitive*
24. The squirrels <u>gathered</u> acorns for their young. *transitive*

25. We <u>grew</u> many different vegetables in the garden. *transitive*
26. The snow <u>fell</u>. *intransitive*
27. Her children never <u>share</u> their toys. *transitive*
28. The band <u>marched</u> in the parade. *intransitive*
29. The children <u>slept</u>. *intransitive*
30. The author <u>sold</u> many books. *transitive*

31. The contractors built a new <u>house</u>.
32. I met the <u>man</u> of my dreams at the party.
33. The porter carried the old woman's <u>luggage</u>.
34. The river flooded the farmer's <u>fields</u>.
35. She chose her best <u>friend</u> as her bridesmaid.

36. The strawberries <u>tasted</u> so sweet.
37. I <u>was</u> ready for the trip.
38. The lilacs in the garden <u>smell</u> sweet.
39. Jack <u>felt</u> nervous about his trip.
40. Mr. McGurn <u>is</u> an editor of a daily newspaper.

CHAPTER 5, ADJECTIVES, p. 18

1. I bought a <u>new</u> <u>green</u> hat.
2. <u>Mary's</u> <u>blue</u> dress is stunning.
3. <u>Some</u> people will help you.
4. The <u>red</u> flowers are on the <u>kitchen</u> table.
5. It was the <u>worst</u> storm of the decade.
6. The <u>farthest</u> distance he ran was <u>ten</u> miles.

7. I love <u>Swiss</u> chocolate. *proper adjective*
8. This stew is <u>great</u>! *predicate adjective*
9. <u>Our</u> house has a fireplace. *possessive adjective*
10. We went to a <u>Hawaiian</u> luau. *proper adjective*
11. <u>Laura's</u> book is damaged. *possessive adjective*
12. Will he stay <u>long</u>? *predicate adjective*

13. The <u>most beautiful</u> sunsets are seen on a beach. *superlative*
14. The truth sounds <u>stranger</u> than fiction. *comparative*
15 That is a <u>pretty</u> dress. *positive*
16. Your first project was <u>more difficult</u> than this one. *comparative*
17. Are you looking for a <u>better</u> job? *comparative*

18. Thank you for the <u>hot</u> meal. *positive*
19. Andy wore his <u>oldest</u> clothes to clean the attic. *superlative*
20. The musician felt <u>more frustrated</u> today than yesterday. *comparative*
21. Jimmy was about to face the <u>most difficult</u> challenge of his life. *superlative*
22. The lamp has a <u>tinted</u> shade. *positive*

CHAPTER 6, ADVERBS, p. 21

1. Silvia is wearing a <u>bright</u> blue dress
2. I have eaten <u>quite</u> <u>enough</u> chocolate cookies.
3. Please listen <u>especially</u> <u>carefully</u> to the instructions.
4. <u>Slowly</u>, the leaves changed their colors.
5. He is <u>always</u> <u>completely</u> prepared for class.

6. You have <u>too</u> many excuses!
   Too modifies many. Many is an adjective.
7. The show was cancelled because <u>too</u> few people bought tickets.
   Too modifies few. Few is an adjective.
8. This is <u>not</u> a difficult task.
   Not modifies difficult. Difficult is an adjective.
9. Our class will <u>never</u> forget this lesson.
   Never modifies will forget. Will forget is a verb.
10. She finished her work <u>earlier</u> than he did.
    Earlier modifies finished. Finished is a verb.
11. Robert spoke <u>very</u> <u>well</u>.
    Very modifies well. Well is an adverb.
    Well modifies spoke. Spoke is a verb.

12. <u>Why</u> is there no school on Monday?
13. <u>When</u> are we going to leave?
14. <u>How</u> is your grandmother feeling?

15. They danced <u>most gracefully</u>. *superlative*
16. The car raced <u>quickly</u> down the road. *positive*
17. Stan practices <u>more seriously</u> than Harry. *comparative*
18. My sister Helen is an <u>unusually</u> smart chess player. *positive*
19. The finish line is <u>farther</u> away than I thought. *comparative*
20. Which of your three brothers runs <u>fastest</u>? *superlative*

CHAPTER 7, PREPOSITIONS, p. 22

1. Sarah had to leave <u>after</u> dinner.
2. She went <u>along with</u> their decision.
3. Ashley and Megan walked <u>on</u> the seashore <u>for</u> hours.
4. Jane gave me the vegetable recipe <u>in addition to</u> the cake recipe.
5. <u>Before</u> his vacation, Matthew read three books.
6. We spent our day <u>at</u> the fair.
7. The woman <u>on</u> my left smiled <u>at</u> you.
8. <u>In spite of</u> the rain, the party was a success.

CHAPTER 8, CONJUNCTIONS, p. 24

1. We will leave <u>as soon as</u> Maria comes downstairs. *subordinating conjunction*
2. I forgot to study for the test; <u>however</u>, I still did well. *conjunctive adverb*
3. Today I saw my friend Adam, <u>and</u> we played a game of basketball. *coordinating conjunction*
4. We will have fun <u>whether</u> we win <u>or</u> lose. *correlative conjunction*
5. <u>Either</u> you <u>or</u> I will have to make dinner tonight. *correlative conjunction*

6. I burned my hand; <u>therefore</u>, I cannot play baseball today.
7. I'm a good swimmer <u>because</u> I've taken swimming lessons for five years.
8. I have a little sister, <u>and</u> Dan has a little sister.
9. You cannot play on the team <u>as long as</u> your grades are poor.
10. We rested at our campsite <u>until</u> the sun rose over the mountain.

CHAPTER 9, INTERJECTIONS, p. 25

1. <u>Whew</u>! It is so humid.
2. <u>Nonsense</u>! I don't believe a word of it.
3. <u>Good</u>! We have finally won.
4. <u>Oh no</u>, the rain will cancel our game.
5. <u>Stop</u>! I can't stand it anymore.

CHAPTER 10, SUBJECT AND PREDICATE, p. 27

1. The maple tree (was twenty feet high.)
2. The sun (rises every morning.)
3. The birds (built their nest.)
4. We (went to the doctor's office.)
5. The small child (stomped his foot.)

6. I (eat) a snack every afternoon.
7. You (knew) how much it would cost.
8. The pond (froze) quickly last winter.
9. They (shook) the sand off their feet.
10. My little brother (has written) his name for the first time.

11. Either <u>Jill</u> or <u>Dan</u> is going to win the contest.
12. <u>Jim</u> and <u>Helen</u> have learned their lessons.
13. Both <u>Los Angeles</u> and <u>San Francisco</u> were shaken by the earthquake.
14. <u>Jeff</u> and <u>Mariko</u> have grown a lot since last summer.
15. Neither <u>you</u> nor the <u>team</u> will practice today.

16. Daniel <u>sneezed</u> and <u>coughed</u>.
17. The boys neither <u>ate</u> nor <u>slept</u>.
18. My father <u>moaned</u> and <u>groaned</u> when his team lost.
19. The students either <u>studied</u> or <u>read</u> in the library.
20. The batter <u>swung</u> and <u>missed</u> the baseball.

CHAPTER 11, COMPLEMENTS, p. 30

1. Lucy will bake a <u>cake</u>. *direct object*
2. Fulton invented the <u>steamboat</u>. *direct object*
3. Barbara will show <u>Ginny</u> her <u>room</u>. Ginny *indirect object*, room *direct object*
4. Aki sent <u>Eileen</u> a <u>present</u>. Eileen *indirect object*, present *direct object*
5. The class named <u>William</u> team <u>leader</u>. William *direct object*, leader *object complement*
6. Your kindness made <u>him</u> <u>happy</u>. him *direct object*, happy *object complement*
7. Cynthia finds <u>chemistry</u> <u>fascinating</u>. chemistry *direct object*, fascinating *object complement*
8. Washington became our first <u>president</u>. *predicate nominative*
9. Our nation's capital is <u>Washington D.C.</u> *predicate nominative*
10. Today's homework seemed <u>easy</u>. *predicate adjective*
11. Phil was <u>hungry</u>. *predicate adjective*
12. Ron is my <u>brother</u>. *predicate adjective*
13. The old man looked <u>grumpy</u>. *predicate adjective*

CHAPTER 12, PHRASES, pp. 34-35

1. <u>Playing in the park</u> is my favorite pastime. *noun*
2. I can be there <u>at eight o'clock</u>. *adverb*
3. The woman <u>in the red dress</u> is very pretty. *adjective*
4. We <u>couldn't have left</u> school any sooner. *verb*
5. The car <u>in the garage</u> is blue. *adjective*
6. Brian likes <u>to read mysteries</u>. *noun*
7. I <u>must not have been</u> the only one absent. *verb*
8. Jean danced <u>with Jim</u>. *adverb*
9. The equipment <u>inside the locker</u> was very valuable. *adjective*
10. <u>To see the new house</u> will be fun. *noun*

11. The star fell <u>from the sky</u>.
12. The school was <u>around the corner</u>.
13. <u>During recess</u> we sell milk and cookies.
14. The trapeze artist performed <u>without a net</u>.
15. The ship was lost <u>beneath the sea</u>.

16. Many immigrants came to America <u>hoping to make their fortunes</u>.
17. <u>Demonstrating ingenuity</u>, the boys sold lemonade on the corner.
18. <u>Looking through my field glasses</u>, I watched the batter strike out.
19. The flowers <u>growing in the park</u> were quite colorful.
20. The car came around the corner, <u>trying to make the light</u>.

21. Donna, <u>a classmate</u>, is a straight A student.
22. My birthday is in June, <u>a summer month</u>.
23. San Diego, <u>my hometown</u>, has nice beaches.
24. My brother <u>Mark</u> can be really annoying.

25. Exercising daily is a good habit.
26. Playing video games is fun.
27. Seeing a rainbow is exhilarating.
28. Swimming laps is relaxing.

29. The dog started to growl fiercely.
30. They had the desire to dance.
31. She was delighted to have won.
32. To learn this material will not be difficult.
33. They chose to live in the suburbs.

34. The task completed, the team took a break.
35. Having planned the activities in advance, we had a great party. *or*
    We had a great party, having planned the activities in advance.
36. Waking up late, he missed the train.
37. The garden, with the lilacs blooming along the pathway, is more fragrant than ever. *or*
    With the lilacs blooming along the pathway, the garden is more fragrant than ever.
38. She wrote her term paper on Asia, hoping to visit one day.

CHAPTER 13, CLAUSES, p. 37

1. Even though it was late, we did not feel tired.
   adverb clause
2. The computer, that I used today, is in the library.
   adjective clause
3. I will interview whichever person runs for office.
   noun clause
4. This is the spot where I lost my watch. *adjective clause*
5. The team left the field after the sun went down.
   adverb clause
6. This is the woman who picked the winning lottery number. *adjective clause*
7. The man who painted our house is a relative of yours.
   adjective clause
8. He will not show me what he painted. *noun clause*
9. As soon as you are ready, the test will begin.
   adverb clause
10. The Statue of Liberty, which I saw last month, is one of my favorite tourist attractions. *adjective clause*
11. He was instructed to begin when the clock struck two.
    adverb clause
12. I did not know that Pike's Peak is in Colorado.
    noun clause
13. Wherever you go, our best wishes will be with you.
    adverb clause

1. Do you want to go out, or shall we stay home?
2. Tom and I laughed, but nobody else thought the joke was funny.
3. She asked Jim and me to join her, but we had other plans.
4. Those keys are mine, and these keys are yours.
5. Jim went to the dentist, and his mother waited in the car.

6. We drove back from our trip last night. The ride took two hours.
7. Whose team will they play next? You and he bought tickets.
8. You and I will bring them to the park. Will their mother be there?
9. I looked for you at the store. We ate lunch without you.
10. What time did you come home? I came home very early.

11. She told a funny joke, and we all laughed. *compound*
12. The girls did not arrive on time but, (because we knew they were coming,) we prepared dinner.
    compound-complex
13. (If it keeps snowing,) I will build a snowman and my friends will build an igloo. *compound-complex*
14. (Although it is sunny,) it is not warm. *complex*
15. Will you stay, or will you go? *compound*
16. The party ended (when the clock struck twelve,) and all the guests went home. *compound-complex*
17. I thought it was the right answer, but the teacher marked it incorrect. *compound*
18. (Although I am afraid of heights,) I went to the top of the Empire State Building and, to my surprise, I enjoyed the view. *compound-complex*
19. (While you are up,) please answer the phone. *complex*
20. I must see the giraffes (whenever I go to the zoo.)
    complex
21. Bernie visited with me (while you were on vacation) but she didn't stay long enough. *compound-complex*

	PRESENT	PRESENT PARTICIPLE	PAST FORM	PAST PARTICIPLE
1.	walk	walking	walked	walked
2.	fall	falling	fell	fallen
3.	put	putting	put	put
4.	run	running	ran	ran
5.	work	working	worked	worked

		PAST FORM	PAST PARTICIPLE
6.	lead	led	led
7.	know	knew	known
8.	choose	chose	chosen
9.	freeze	froze	frozen
10.	grow	grew	grown
11.	shake	shook	shaken
12.	swing	swung	swung
13.	tear	tore	torn
14.	shine	shone	shone
15.	bring	brought	brought
16.	drink	drank	drunk
17.	forget	forgot	forgotten
18.	go	went	gone
19.	lend	lent	lent
20.	lie	lay	lain
21.	run	ran	run
22.	ride	rode	ridden
23.	ring	rang	rung
24.	speed	sped	sped
25.	swim	swam	swum
26.	take	took	taken

CHAPTER 16, TENSE OF VERBS, pp. 46-48

1. They <u>move</u> the furniture every few months.
2. The family <u>plans</u> a long vacation.
3. Pierina <u>loves</u> her little brother.
4. The bright girl <u>answers</u> difficult questions.
5. Dennis <u>learns</u> basic social studies.

6. Mark <u>bounced</u> the ball.
7. I <u>was</u> happy.
8. Shane and Connor <u>liked</u> those cookies.
9. Mike <u>played</u> with his new puppy.
10. Diane <u>walked</u> all the way home.

11. She <u>will turn</u> the pages for the pianist at the concert.
12. The mother <u>will bake</u> chocolate cookies for the children.
13. We <u>are going to use</u> new art supplies for the project.
14. My best friend <u>will buy</u> tickets for both of us.
15. I <u>will work</u> on my report this weekend.

16. The girls <u>have seen</u> this movie.
17. She <u>has talked</u> for two hours.
18. Jennifer <u>has jumped</u> rope.
19. My parents <u>have driven</u> to Canada.
20. Tim <u>has drawn</u> the colorful pictures.

21. My neighbor's dog <u>barked</u> all night long. *past tense*
22. I <u>shall explain</u> the lesson again. *future tense*
23. Silvia <u>works</u> very hard on her papers. *present tense*
24. Albert, please <u>shut</u> the door now. *present tense*
25. The lecturer <u>talked</u> for nearly two hours. *past tense*

26. The flowers <u>bloomed</u> last June.
27. Manny, please <u>walk</u> to the store right now.
28. No one <u>stands</u> on the stage.
29. The high school team <u>plays</u> football every year.
30. Yesterday, Louisa <u>recited</u> her piece very well.

31. As of April fifteenth, she <u>will have worked</u> here one year. *future perfect*
32. Abe <u>has gone</u> to the store. *present perfect*
33. She <u>had studied</u> Latin before she took French. *past perfect*
34. The game <u>will have started</u> by the time we get there. *future perfect*
35. Before the restoration began, Mr. Jones <u>had bought</u> the house. *past perfect*
36. Maria <u>will have planted</u> all the flowers before I get back. *future perfect*
37. Ben and Jerry <u>have made</u> a mess. *present perfect*
38. By tomorrow you <u>will have sailed</u> to the island. *future perfect*
39. He told me what I <u>had told</u> you earlier. *past perfect*
40. After this hike, David <u>will have walked</u> ten miles. *future perfect*

41. Jill <u>does grow</u> beautiful flowers.
42. Pete <u>does ride</u> the bike fast.
43. The children <u>do smile</u> often.
44. The baby <u>does play</u> with his toy.
45. My grandmother <u>does sleep</u> soundly.

46. The band played loudly, and the couples <u>danced</u>.
47. The comedian telling funny jokes makes the audience <u>laugh</u>.
48. The sun set over the hills before the rain <u>fell</u>.
49. When I get hungry, I <u>have</u> a snack.
50. John crossed the finish line first, and his coach <u>cheered</u>.

CHAPTER 17, VERB VOICE AND MOOD, p. 50

1. The teenager <u>watched</u> the teacher. *active voice*
2. The glass <u>was broken</u>. *passive voice*
3. Jennifer <u>finished</u> third in the race. *active voice*
4. The children <u>rode</u> the pony all afternoon. *active voice*
5. The tent <u>was pitched</u> by the scout leader. *passive voice*
6. The race <u>was won</u> by our team. *passive voice*
7. Mary <u>sang</u> in the choir. *active voice*
8. They <u>caught</u> the bus to the store. *active voice*
9. The garden <u>was planted</u> by Mike. *passive voice*
10. The dinner <u>was prepared</u> by Sheila. *passive voice*

11. Please <u>clean</u> your room. *imperative mood*
12. Joseph <u>got</u> an A on his exam. *indicative mood*
13. <u>May</u> the better player <u>win</u>. *subjunctive mood*

14. <u>Keep</u> an eye on the dog. *imperative mood*
15. The trip to the zoo <u>was</u> fun. *indicative mood*
16. I <u>recommend</u> that you arrive early. *subjunctive mood*
17. <u>Did</u> you <u>see</u> that? *indicative mood*
18. <u>Study</u> for your test. *imperative mood*
19. My canary <u>sings</u> sweetly. *indicative mood*
20. It <u>would be</u> wise to pack lightly. *subjunctive mood*

CHAPTER 18, SUBJECT & VERB AGREEMENT, p.53

1. Ham and eggs <u>is</u> my favorite breakfast.
2. Mark and Alan <u>are</u> going to the movies.
3. Neither my brother nor sister <u>is</u> home.
4. His pants <u>are</u> blue.
5. Neither the team nor the coach <u>likes</u> to play in the rain.
6. Andrea, along with the other flutists, <u>hopes</u> to qualify for the contest.
7. The family <u>goes</u> on a picnic.
8. Jack, Tim, and Bob <u>receive</u> their allowance every Monday.
9. Four hours <u>is</u> too long to wait on line.
10. Fifteen dollars <u>is</u> the price of the shirt.
11. Half of the tickets <u>were</u> sold.
12. Attaining good grades <u>shows</u> that you learned your lessons.
13. Tom's paintings are the most beautiful that <u>have</u> been displayed.
14. Social studies <u>is</u> the subject scheduled for the first period.
15. The bunch of bananas <u>is</u> hanging from the tree.

CHAPTER 19, MODIFYING CORRECTLY, p.56

1. Rose always does <u>good</u> work.
2. I was <u>badly</u> frightened by that story.
3. You drew those posters very <u>well</u>.
4. I felt very <u>bad</u> when I learned you were ill.
5. It's a <u>good</u> thing you brought an umbrella.

6. She was not able to tell <u>anybody</u> about the surprise.
7. I never went <u>anywhere</u> outside the United States.
8. He didn't do <u>anything</u> for the club.
9. She wasn't <u>anywhere</u> near the finish line.
10. He can't do <u>anything</u> right.

11. While I was putting the turkey in the oven, the phone rang.
12. I borrowed a radio with an antenna from my sister.
13. When I was five years old, my father taught me to play baseball. *or*
    My father taught me to play baseball when I was five years old.
14. Standing on our toes, we watched the ballerina. *or*
    Standing on her toes, she watched the ballerina. *or*
    We watched the ballerina as she stood on her toes.

15. I read in this morning's paper about the thieves who were captured. *or*
    In this morning's paper, I read about the thieves who were captured.
16. I could not find the butter on the bottom shelf of the refrigerator. *or*
    I could not find the butter because it was on the bottom shelf of the refrigerator. *or*
    I looked on the bottom shelf of the refrigerator, but I could not find the butter.

CHAPTER 23, PARAGRAPHS, p.77

1, 8, 14

The text should be divided into three paragraphs. The first describes what the Hernandez children did while they were in the park. The second paragraph, beginning with "Later that day, they went..." tells about the process of choosing and seeing a movie. The third paragraph, beginning with the words, "The Hernandez family went to..." describes the dinner the family ate that evening.

INDEX

INDEX